Smoking

Other Books of Related Interest

Teen Decisions Series
Alcohol
Pregnancy
Sex
Violence

Opposing Viewpoints Series
Addiction
Chemical Dependency
Opposing Viewpoints in Social Issues
Teens at Risk
Tobacco and Smoking

Current Controversies Series
Smoking
Teen Addiction

Contemporary Issues Companions Series
Cancer
Teen Smoking

At Issue Series
Marijuana
Smoking

Smoking

Laura K. Egendorf, *Book Editor*

David L. Bender, *Publisher*

Bruno Leone, *Executive Editor*

Bonnie Szumski, *Editorial Director*

Stuart B. Miller, *Managing Editor*

James D. Torr, *Series Editor*

Greenhaven Press Inc., San Diego, California

Teen
Decisions

No part of this book may be reproduced or used in any form or by any means, electrical, mechanical, or otherwise, including, but not limited to, photocopy, recording, or any information storage and retrieval system, without prior written permission from the publisher.

Every effort has been made to trace owners of copyrighted material.

Library of Congress Cataloging-in-Publication Data

Smoking / Laura K. Egendorf, book editor.
        p. cm. — (Teen decisions)
    Includes bibliographical references and index.
    ISBN 0-7377-0495-0 (pbk. : alk. paper) —
    ISBN 0-7377-0496-9 (lib. bdg. : alk. paper)
    1. Teenagers—Tobacco use—United States. 2. Tobacco habit—
United States. 3. Smoking—United States. I. Egendorf, Laura K.,
1973–   . II. Series.

HV5745 .S53   2001
362.29'6'0973—dc21
                                                            00-037671
                                                                 CIP

Cover Photo: © Michael Krasowitz/FPG

© 2001 by Greenhaven Press, Inc.
PO Box 289009, San Diego, CA 92198-9009

Printed in the U.S.A.

Contents

Foreword   7
Introduction   9

Chapter 1: Why Teens Smoke
1. Personality Traits of Teen Smokers   19
   Janet Brigham

2. Smoking and the Teenage Mind   24
   Marshall Brain

3. Why Teenage Girls Are More Vulnerable to   30
   Smoking
   Mimi Frost and Susan Baxter

4. Explaining the Rise in Smoking Among African   37
   American Teenagers
   Phillip Gardiner

Point of Contention: Does Advertising Encourage   42
Teens to Smoke?
   America *and Jacob Sullum*

Chapter 2: Perspectives on Teen Smoking
1. Four Teens Share Their Views   51
   Brandi Battle, Kellie Jolly, Nickita Bradley,
   and Josh

2. Regrets of Teen Smokers   61
   Patricia J. Murphy

3. A Former Smoker Looks Back   67
   Dale Pray

4. Not Ready to Quit 72
   Kevin Simpson

5. Dealing with a Family of Smokers 77
   Trenée Bryant Broughton

Chapter 3: The Effects of Smoking
1. Smoking Has Serious Health Effects 83
   Paul H. Brodish

2. The Dangers of Smokeless Tobacco 93
   KidsHealth.org

3. Smoking Does Not Cause Weight Loss 98
   Sandra G. Boodman

Point of Contention: Is Smoking a Bad Habit or 102
an Addiction?
   Action on Smoking and Health and Judith Hatton

Chapter 4: Responses to Teen Smoking
1. How to Quit 111
   National Cancer Institute

2. Teens' Views on Government Anti-Tobacco 118
   Efforts
   Susan Page and Wendy Koch

3. Teens Can Take Action 125
   Patricia Sosa

Bibliography 131
Organizations to Contact 135
Index 140

Foreword

The teen years are a time of transition from childhood to adulthood. By age thirteen, most teenagers have started the process of physical growth and sexual maturation that enables them to produce children of their own. In the United States and other industrialized nations, teens who have entered or completed puberty are still children in the eyes of the law. They remain the responsibility of their parents or guardians and are not expected to make major decisions themselves. In most of the United States, eighteen is the age of legal adulthood. However, in some states, the age of majority is nineteen, and some legal restrictions on adult activities, such as drinking alcohol, extend until age twenty-one.

This prolonged period between the onset of puberty and the achieving of legal adulthood is not just a matter of hormonal and physical change, but a learning process as well. Teens must learn to cope with influences outside the immediate family. For many teens, friends or peer groups become the basis for many of their opinions and actions. In addition, teens are influenced by TV shows, advertising, and music.

The *Teen Decisions* series aims at helping teens make responsible choices. Each book provides readers with thought-provoking advice and information from a variety of perspectives. Most of the articles in these anthologies were originally written for, and in many cases by, teens. Some of the essays focus on ethical and moral dilemmas, while others present pertinent legal and scientific information. Many of the articles tell personal stories about decisions teens have made and how their lives were affected.

One special feature of this series is the "Points of Contention," in which specially paired articles present directly opposing views on controversial topics. Additional features in each book include a listing of organizations to contact for more information, as well as a bibliography to aid readers interested in more information. The *Teen Decisions* series strives to include both trustworthy information and multiple opinions on topics important to teens, while respecting the role teens play in making their own choices.

Introduction

Tobacco has been a major American crop for more than two thousand years. It was used originally by Native Americans and brought back to Europe by Christopher Columbus. Because it was so plentiful, tobacco was used as money in the British colonies in the 1600s and helped finance the Revolutionary War. And when it has not been used as currency, tobacco has been smoked or chewed. The tobacco product we are most familiar with—cigarettes—started to gain popularity in the early 1900s. Among the brands introduced during that time was Camel, which the R.J. Reynolds Tobacco Company first sold in 1913. Today, approximately 50 million Americans smoke, including 25 percent of Americans over eighteen.

But smoking is not limited to adults—statistics indicate that it is likely that you or a classmate have tried smoking and perhaps continue to do so. According to a January 2000 survey that was conducted by the Centers for Disease Control and Prevention and the American Legacy Foundation, 12.8 percent of middle school students and 34.8 percent of high school students in the United States use tobacco products, most commonly cigarettes. Teenagers who smoke give a variety of reasons for their habit—peer pressure caused by friends who smoke, a desire to appear mature, or rebellion against parents. Another explanation that has been offered, particularly by critics of teen smoking, is the effect of advertising. The impact of tobacco advertising on teens and its influence on their pursuit of the habit has been a long-standing controversy.

Cigarette Advertising: The Early Years

Tobacco products have been advertised throughout the twentieth century. Odd as it may sound today, when surgeon general warnings are a required element of cigarette ads, tobacco advertising prior to the 1960s positioned cigarettes as a healthy activity. A popular claim for cigarettes in the first half of the twentieth century was that they caused less throat irritation than their competitors. Doctors and nurses endorsed different brands; a 1936 ad stated "more doctors smoke Camels than any other cigarette." From 1933 to 1953, the *Journal of the American Medical Association* published cigarette advertisements. Besides seeking the approval of the medical establishment, tobacco companies also used celebrities in their ads as a way to make smoking seem glamorous. Among the notable faces in cigarette ads were baseball legend Joe DiMaggio and then–movie star Ronald Reagan.

In the 1920s, tobacco companies began to target women. Until World War I, female smoking had been seen as inappropriate—an activity associated with "loose" women. But according to an article in the journal *Tobacco Control*, women began to take on new roles and attitudes during the war. Amanda Amosa and Margaretha Haglund, the authors of the article, "From Social Taboo to 'Torch of Freedom': The Marketing of Cigarettes to Women," explain:

> The first world war proved to be a watershed in both the emancipation of women and the spread of smoking among women. During the war many women had not only taken on "male" occupations but had also started to wear trousers, play sports, cut their hair, and smoke. Subsequently attitudes towards women smoking began to change, and more and more women started to use the cigarette as a weapon in their increasing challenge to traditional ideas about female behaviour.

According to Amosa and Haglund, tobacco companies exploited the notions of power and liberation in their cigarette ads of the 1920s and 1930s. These companies also took advantage of women's desire to be thin—showing that some things never change, because the belief that smoking will prevent weight gain is one factor that drives many teenage girls to take up the habit today. Amosa and Haglund note that American Tobacco Company's Lucky Strike brand more than doubled its market share through its "Reach for Lucky Instead of a Sweet" campaign. In addition, Philip Morris marketed Marlboro as a woman's cigarette. According to the Community Outreach Health Information System (COHIS), based at the Boston University Medical Center, the smoking rates of female teenagers tripled between 1925 and 1935 as a result of these advertisements. (For many decades, sixteen and seventeen-year-olds were legally permitted to, if not purchase, then at least use cigarettes.) Virginia Slims, the brand most closely associated with women—and, many argue, teenage girls—would not appear in the marketplace until 1968.

Criticisms of Cigarettes

After reading about these early cigarette advertisements, you might be wondering if anyone questioned the health effects of tobacco. In fact, criticism of smoking is nearly as old as the habit. In 1604, King James I declared: "Smoking is a custom loathsome to the eye, hateful to the nose, harmful to the brain, and dangerous to the lungs." In 1892, the Senate Committee on Epidemic Diseases declared cigarettes a public health hazard. By the 1920s—the same time as cigarette ads began to proliferate—studies started to link lung cancer and smoking. These studies culminated on January 11, 1964, when Surgeon General Luther L. Terry released the report of the Surgeon General's Advisory Committee on Smoking and Health. On the basis of more than 7,000 studies, the report concluded that smoking causes lung cancer, laryngeal cancer, and chronic bronchitis. Armed with that knowledge, the federal government began to take steps to restrict tobacco company advertising. In 1965, the Federal Cigarette Labeling and Advertising Act required that surgeon general's warnings be placed on cigarette packs. In 1971, broadcast ads for cigarettes were banned.

The focus of these restrictions, from 1971 to today, is the belief that cigarette companies are targeting teenagers. This belief has been supported by studies that have concluded that cigarette advertising is a major factor in teenagers' decision to smoke. In February 1998, a study was published in the *Journal of the American Medical Association* which concluded that approximately one-third of the adolescents who experiment with tobacco do so because of promotional activities. Not coincidentally, the most-advertised brands are also the ones that teenagers are most likely to smoke. According to the Campaign for Tobacco-Free Kids, "Eighty-six percent of kids who smoke (but only about a third of adults) prefer Marlboro, Camel and Newport—the three most heavily advertised brands. Marlboro, the most heavily advertised brand, controls almost 60 percent of the youth market."

Targeting Teenagers

Deciding whether to smoke is an issue with which most teens grapple, and critics of tobacco advertising charge that teenagers cannot make an informed choice if they are constantly bombarded with magazine ads, billboards, and promotions that present smoking as a fun and cool activity. This criticism is supported by tobacco company documents from the 1970s and 1980s, which show that youths have been targeted as a key market. An R. J. Reynolds memorandum from 1975 (which was not released until 1997) states: "To ensure increased and longer-term growth for the Camel Filter, the brand must increase its share penetration among the 14–24 age group."

One way to increase market share among teens is to develop tobacco products that will appeal to young tastes. For example, chewing tobacco comes in mint and cherry flavors; a Skoal executive even acknowledged in a 1984 *Wall Street Journal* article that "cherry Skoal is for somebody who likes the taste of candy, if you know what I'm saying." In 1992, the tobacco company Brown and Williamson considered selling tobacco-based lollipops, fruit rollups, and other sweets.

Another way that tobacco companies have allegedly targeted teenagers is by developing advertising campaigns that appeal to the youthful desire to be trendy and in style. One campaign you may be familiar with centered around the cartoon figure Joe Camel. More than any other cigarette campaign, Joe Camel has been accused of enticing children and teenagers into smoking. The Joe Camel campaign, which featured a sunglasses-wearing and saxophone-playing cartoon camel, "Old Joe," in its print advertisements, was launched in 1987. Joe Camel quickly became recognizable among even young children. A 1991 survey discovered that a staggering 91 percent of the six-year-olds queried not only recognized Joe but associated him with cigarettes. The same percentage recognized Mickey Mouse's silhouette. Though these six-year-olds probably didn't begin smoking Camels as a result of the advertising, their older brothers and sisters may have—in just three years, Camel's share of the under-eighteen market shot up from less than 1 percent to 33 percent.

Another way that Camel was able to garner such a large proportion of the youth market, charge anti-smoking activists, was through promotions offered in magazines with significant youth readerships, such as *Rolling Stone*. The "Camel Cash" campaign began in 1991, offering coupons for merchandise in every pack. The coupons could then be redeemed for Joe Camel merchandise—T-shirts, baseball caps, jackets, and other goods that arguably would be found more appealing by a 16-year-old boy than someone twice his age. In this view, the desire to acquire fashionable clothes—to look as cool as Joe Camel did in his ads—became another reason why teenagers had to struggle with whether to smoke. Teenagers want to be cool, and if the advertisements in their favorite magazines link smoking with fashion and style, and their friends are walking around in Joe Camel base-ball caps, then the desire to smoke can become even stronger.

If you want to link fashion and smoking, though, a better choice than Joe Camel might be Virginia Slims, a product of Philip Morris. Launched in 1968 as a woman's brand, it quickly became the favorite cigarette of teenage girls. By 1974, the number of teenage girls who smoked had doubled. Teenage girls are sometimes tempted to smoke because they think it will help them keep off weight and look more sophisticated; the word "slim" in the brand name might be seen as accentuating that belief. Virginia Slims ads, with their photos of spirited young women, capitalize on the desires of these girls, as do their fashion promotions, with items that include backpacks and sunglasses.

Movies and Sports

Another problem that anti-smoking activists have is that, even though television ads for cigarettes have been banned since 1971, tobacco companies are still able to advertise their wares on television by sponsoring sporting events. Until 1996, Virginia Slims was a sponsor of the women's tennis tour. R. J. Reynolds sponsors Winston Cup auto racing and tobacco company names are regularly festooned on race cars. Tobacco billboards are a regular feature at baseball games and can often be seen in television broadcasts.

Cigarettes are prominent on the big screen as well—if movies were real life, you might think that everyone smokes. In 1997, the University of California at San Francisco released a study showing that 77 percent of the movies made in 1996 included at least one tobacco-related scene. More important is which characters smoked—namely, the successful and attractive lead characters. Between 1991 and 1996, 80 percent of the male leads and 27 percent of the female leads smoked. Teens watching their favorite actors and actresses might readily associate smoking with success and heroism. Freelance writer Christine H. Rowley notes: "Smoking is decreasing among adults, but increasing among pre-teens and teens." She maintains that "this will continue on an upward spiral as long as smoking in film continues on its present pervasive levels."

The Government Takes Action

In the mid-1990s, federal and state governments began making concerted efforts to end tobacco company's marketing to youths. In August 1996, President Clinton announced a program to prevent kids from using tobacco. The program would give the Federal Drug Administration (FDA) the power to regulate tobacco advertising and promotions; promotional items, brand-name sponsorship of sports events, and other advertising that might appeal to minors would be prohibited. "Would" being the operative word—a district judge ruled in April 1997 that the FDA lacked such authority. The Clinton administration appealed the ruling, sending the case to the Supreme Court. On March 21, 2000, the Supreme Court ruled by a 5-4 decision that the FDA lacks the authority to regulate tobacco as an addictive drug.

However, in November 1998, the tobacco industry settled a lawsuit with forty-six states, agreeing to pay $206 billion, submit to advertising regulations, and fund an anti-smoking campaign. The companies were also forbidden from sponsoring sports events or teams with underage participants. The states had sued the major tobacco companies in order to recoup the health-care costs of treating diseases caused by tobacco consumption. Among the results of this settlement is R.J. Reynolds ceasing sponsorship of car races where sixteen and seventeen-year-olds could participate. Even Joe Camel could not survive, when R.J. Reynolds agreed in July 1997 to end that particular campaign.

Other government efforts to limit tobacco advertising have not been so successful. Congress, despite several attempts, has not yet approved a bill that would regulate tobacco marketing. In June 1998, the Senate rejected a bill by Republican senator

John McCain that would have banned outdoor advertising and the use of cartoon figures, animals, and humans in ads.

Questioning the Influence of Cigarette Advertising

In contrast to all the criticisms of tobacco advertising, some studies suggest that advertising does *not* cause teens to smoke. For example, the magazine *Scholastic Update* noted in February 1996 that 97 percent of teens surveyed in one poll said that advertising does not influence their decision to smoke. The magazine quotes one teen, Amanda Novak, as saying, "'I see those ads and I just laugh because they are so unrealistic and stupid.'" Jacob Sullum, senior editor for *Reason*, notes that the same survey, which revealed the wide recognition six-year-olds have for Joe Camel, also showed that those same children do not have a positive view of smoking—85 percent of the children surveyed had a negative attitude toward cigarettes.

Sullum also posits that while advertising might encourage teens to smoke particular brands of cigarettes, studies have yet to prove conclusively that those ads lead to a general rise in teen smoking. He writes that anti-smoking activists do not "acknowledge that tobacco companies could be competing for new smokers without actually creating them. Although the companies deny that they target minors in any way, building brand loyalty among teenagers is still not the same thing as making them into smokers."

According to Sullum, teenagers who smoke and view tobacco advertisements and promotional products favorably most likely begin smoking for other reasons. Wanda Hamilton, writing for the National Smokers Alliance, takes a different tact. She argues that if advertising did lead to teen smoking, then the restrictions on advertisements that began in 1971 would have resulted in a decline in teen smoking. Instead, notes Hamilton, the rate has remained relatively high and constant, hovering around 30 percent for most years until a sharp increase that began in 1993.

Exploring the Issues of Teen Smoking

Even though tobacco companies spend $5.5 billion each year promoting their products, advertising is not the only reason, or necessarily the biggest reason, why so many teenagers smoke. Others reasons for smoking might include wanting to control one's weight, fit in with a group of friends, or feel like an adult. The reasons why some teenagers decide to smoke, and the impact that decision can have, are explored in *Teen Decisions: Smoking*. In Chapter One, Why Teens Smoke, the authors provide some explanations for teen smoking, such as peer influence and certain personality traits. Chapter Two, Perspectives on Teen Smoking, offers the views of current and former teen smokers, as well as teenagers who never began smoking. They explain why they smoke, why they quit, or why they never started. In Chapter Three, The Effects of Smoking, the contributors detail the health effects of cigarettes and smokeless tobacco and whether smoking can be considered an addiction. Chapter Four, Responses to Teen Smoking, examines ways that teenagers, the government, and businesses can reduce the incidence of teen smoking. These issues are all critical, because the decision of whether to start smoking is one that is usually faced at a young age— the vast majority of smokers start before they turn twenty. It is hoped that *Teen Decisions: Smoking* will provide you with the information you need to make that decision.

Chapter 1

Why Teens Smoke

Personality Traits of Teen Smokers

Janet Brigham

Researchers try to study the habits of teen smokers to find patterns of behavior. Author Janet Brigham cites studies that show smokers are likely to choose certain peer groups, such as heavy metal fans or skateboarders, or have at least one parent that smokes. Teen smokers also tend to exhibit signs of depression, feelings of incompetence, and a desire to cope with stress. Brigham is the author of *Dying to Quit: Why We Smoke and How We Stop*.

Just what draws a young person toward tobacco? If we had better answers to that question, perhaps we would have better ways to prevent pediatric tobacco use in the first place. Sometimes, it can help to reverse the question and determine what draws people *away from* tobacco. For example, the state of Utah, which is heavily populated by persons with a religious prohibition against smoking (Mormons), has the nation's lowest adult smoking rate at 13 percent. Even though Utah ranks low in youth cigarette use, some 44 percent of female and 52 percent of male Utah high school students have tried smoking. Those figures are lower than similar data from other states, but they still represent a substantial number of young persons. Fewer

Utah youths reported current smoking when questioned for a 1995 survey (17 percent for both females and males), and less than half of those were considered frequent users. The teen smoking rates in neighboring Wyoming were more than double those of Utah, and in Nevada they were nearly double.

Does the anti-tobacco religious influence cause these regional differences? Is the youth smoking rate lower among children who are less exposed to adult use of tobacco? In contrast to the other western United States statistics, a greater percentage of young people in California reported having tried tobacco (63 percent of females and 65 percent of males), but only 7 percent of females and 8 percent of males were frequent cigarette users. Smokeless tobacco rates among young persons were also lower in California than in Utah. While California does have a sizable number of Mormons and other nonsmoking groups, such as Seventh Day Adventists, their representation among the overall state population is not sufficient to swing the numbers that dramatically. A more likely explanation is the aggressive anti-tobacco campaigns carried on in California in recent years, coupled with the basic California ardor for health.

A 1998 longitudinal report concluded that advertisements and promotions lead one-third of teenagers to try tobacco. John P. Pierce and his colleagues interviewed a sample of nonsmoking California adolescents in 1993 and re-interviewed them again in 1996. Although the teenagers stated in 1993 that they had no intention of smoking, those who had a favorite cigarette advertisement in 1993 were twice as likely to later start smoking or be willing to start as were those with no favorite ad. Those owning or willing to use a tobacco promotional item in 1993 were nearly three times as likely to be smoking by 1996 as those who were unwilling to use a promotional item.

> Advertisements and promotions lead one-third of teenagers to try tobacco.

About half of the nearly 1,600 teenagers sampled moved closer to becoming smokers between 1993 and 1996. Nearly 30 percent had experimented with smoking during the three-year interval. Of those who expressed a preference for a favorite ad in the first interview, 83 percent favored Camel or Marlboro.

The Influence of Peers

Also, what pulls children and adolescents toward or away from smoking differs from group to group. Reports from Gilbert Botvin and colleagues at Cornell and Columbia universities, who studied predictors of smoking among inner-city Latino and African-American youth, indicated that the most important social influences promoting smoking were friends and peers. Additionally, feelings of hopelessness, lack of efficacy in basic life skills, and low self-esteem appeared to contribute to the likelihood of smoking. In this research, measures of socioeconomic status were unrelated to the extent of smoking. These reports are particularly pertinent because smoking rates among African-American youth are lower than the rates for whites until the trend flip-flops as both groups reach adulthood, when whites' smoking rates fall below those of African-Americans.

The concept of "group self-identification" has also been used to predict adolescent cigarette smoking. A longitudinal study by Steve Sussman and colleagues at the University of Southern California and the University of Illinois at Chicago noted that the peer groups with which seventh graders identified themselves predicted (statistically) smoking in eighth grade. These were the group categories as derived from previous self-descriptions by youth: (1) high-risk youth, including stoners, heavy metalers, and bad kids; (2) skaters, including skaters and surfers; (3) hotshots, including brains and socials; (4) jocks, composed of jocks and cheerleaders; (5) regulars, including new wavers and actors; and (6) others. The highest rate of smoking was among the high-risk youth. Although group self-identification and seventh-grade smoking did significantly predict smoking a year later, the authors were careful to clarify that self-identification was "a fair predictor" with its own merits, but it did not describe the total picture.

Smoking and Personality

The predictive relationship between smoking and the negative emotions of depression or anxiety has been the object of considerable research in adults, but fewer studies have examined it in children and youth. Paul Rohde and a research team at the Oregon Research Institute determined that adolescents who had experienced an episode of depression experienced "psycho-social scars" that included cigarette smoking, in addition to increased health problems and excessive emotional reliance on others. "One implication is that although the rate of smoking in the general population may be decreasing, it may be increasing in adolescents who have experienced an episode of depression," they wrote. "Another possibility . . . is that . . . depressed adolescents progress from experimentation to more serious levels of tobacco use."

Children's competence and their parents' behaviors were linked to early tobacco use in research reported by Christine Jackson at the University of North Carolina at Chapel Hill and her colleagues. They found that children who rated themselves as less competent and whose teachers also rated them as less competent were more likely to use tobacco at an early age. Children were also more likely to use tobacco at

> Feelings of hopelessness, lack of efficacy in basic life skills, and low self-esteem appeared to contribute to the likelihood of smoking.

an early age if their parents were nonaccepting and if their parents were less skilled at setting rules and supervising behavior. Additionally, children of at least one smoking parent were twice as likely to smoke as were their peers whose parents did not smoke.

Children's personality styles at ages six and ten contributed to early use of cigarettes, according to research by Louise Mâsse at the University of Texas-Houston and Richard Tremblay at the University of Montreal. They found that "novelty-seeking" and "low harm avoidance" predicted the early use of tobacco and other substances. They were investigating dimensions of personality postulated by Robert Cloninger in the 1980s.

> Children's personality styles at ages six and ten [contribute] to early use of cigarettes.

Novelty-seeking is believed to be an inherited tendency toward "exploratory activity and exhilaration" prompted by novelty, or by things that appeal to the appetites. *Harm avoidance* refers to an inherited tendency to "react intensively to aversive stimuli," which controls the learning mechanisms that enable inhibition.

Scientists attempting to understand the onset of tobacco use also watch for trigger events and environmental risk factors, in addition to vulnerable personality styles. Young smokers themselves state that they smoke because they enjoy it. A survey of more than 10,000 British adolescents, questioned by J.R. Eisner and colleagues in the 1980s, found that they attributed their cigarette use to the experience of smoking itself, rather than to peer pressure. They said that they found smoking to be an enjoyable, calming act that helped them deal with stress. They were more inclined to reject notions that they were smoking because it was a grown-up thing to do, or because of how it made them look among their peers.

University of Reading, England, researchers David Warburton and colleagues in 1991 summarized such findings to date: "It may not be simple exposure to nicotine that results in adolescent smoking, but that smoking results from the situations in which the young people find themselves at this most stressful time of life." The scientists identified smoking as "a coping strategy" for both younger and older smokers.

Smoking and the Teenage Mind

Marshall Brain

Almost no one begins smoking after he or she has turned twenty. Instead, most take up the habit as teenagers. Marshall Brain, the author of *The Teenager's Guide to the Real World*, asserts that teenagers smoke because their minds work differently from adults. The teenage mind does not stop to consider options, Brain writes, but instead reacts immediately to the situation around it. If teens gave more thoughtful consideration to the decision of whether to smoke, Brain insists, then almost no one would develop the habit.

Why do teenagers start smoking? If you ask teenagers, here are the four most common reasons:

1. Peer pressure, group acceptance—if their friends smoke, many teenagers will begin smoking simply to maintain their acceptance within the group.

2. Image projection—there is definitely an "image" attached to smoking by advertising. For women it is one of sexiness and desirability, and for men it is one of rugged individualism, fun or coolness. If a teenager buys into that image, then smoking begins.

3. Rebellion—many teenagers take up smoking because they

Reprinted from Marshall Brain, "For Teenagers: Understanding Smoking," an online article found at www.bygpub.com/books/tg2rw/smoking.html. Reprinted with permission from BYG Publishing, Inc.

know it annoys/bothers/infuriates their parents and other adults. There is also a certain element of "doing what is not allowed" or "walking on the wild side" worked in as well.

4. Adult aspirations—some teenagers believe that by smoking they are acting like an adult. If the teenager is raised in a community where most of the adults smoke, then this is perhaps a logical conclusion.

The Teenage Mind

There is one other factor at work as well, and most teenagers have no idea it is happening. This factor is the teenage mind itself. The following graph is interesting:

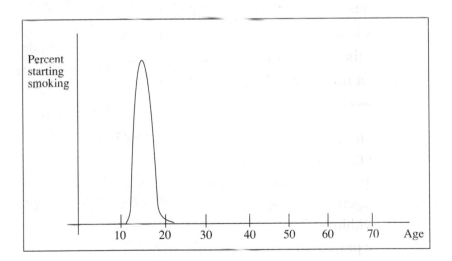

What this graph shows is the age at which people begin smoking. On this graph you can see that some 11 and 12 year-olds start, but in general the ages 13 through 18 are the big "start smoking" years—nearly everyone who starts smoking starts between these ages. Here is the important thing to notice: *No one starts smoking after age 20 or so.* That is, if you can make it to age 20 without smoking, you will never start. This is an extremely interesting fact of life. *No* adult ever makes the decision to smoke. The question to ask yourself as a teenager is "why is that?"

You may find this hard to believe, but the "teenage mind" is much different from the "adult mind." All teenagers eventually figure this out—that is the point at which they start to become adults. But until a teenager turns on his or her adult brain and begins thinking like an adult, he or she is stuck with a teenage brain. The key concept here is that "being a teenager" is a temporary state meant to be outgrown. In other words, "being a teenager" can be equated to "being a child" at some level. The idea is for a teenager to outgrow teendom and become an *adult*.

> Many teenagers take up smoking because they know it annoys/bothers/infuriates their parents and other adults.

Once you understand that, you are on your way. But before that happens your "teenage mind" tends to be extremely non-rational and very reactive. Every single person who starts smoking is doing it because they are using their "teenage mind" to make the decision, rather than an adult mind.

[Note: If you are a teenager reading this article and you are thinking, "Wow, smoking is really stupid—I don't see why anyone ever starts," then that means your adult brain has already started to turn on. Congratulations!]

You can understand the difference between the teenage mind and the adult mind by looking at these two examples:

• Teenage mind: "A couple of my friends have started smoking. I better start too or they will think I am uncool."

• Adult mind: "A couple of my friends have started smoking. Do I want to start smoking?"

Comparing the Adult and Teenage Minds

The difference is that the teenage mind *reacts,* while the adult mind *asks* and *considers options.* You, as a teenager, are a blank slate. You, and only you, get to determine exactly how your life will turn out. You get to choose exactly what appears on your slate by making choices from a nearly infinite pool. In other words, *you get to design your life!* You get to decide on things like:

- What will I choose for my career?
- How much money will I make, and why?
- Who will I marry?
- How many children will I have?
- How will I dress?
- Where will I live?
- What kind of car will I drive?
- Will I go to college, and if so which one will I attend?
- What will be my major in college?
- What will be my attitude toward life?
- What will be my values?
- *Will I smoke? Will I take drugs?*
- What sports do I want to play?
- And so on . . .

However, you only get to *choose* if you think about these things and make conscious choices. The problem for many teenagers, and for nearly every teenager who smokes, is that the choices are not conscious decisions—they are reactions. You can go back and change many of these decisions later, but smoking is not one of them because smoking is addictive.

This fact of life helps answer the following important question: If no adult using their adult brain would ever start smoking, then why do you see millions of adults smoking everywhere you go? The reason is simple: *Every adult smoker started smoking as a teenager because of a silly decision made by their teenage brain, but once addicted to cigarettes it is impossible to stop!* That is the *only* reason you see adult smokers. No one in their right mind (that excludes, of course, a teenager using a teenager mind) would smoke if they didn't have to. But cigarettes are highly addictive so adult smok-

> Until a teenager turns on his or her adult brain and begins thinking like an adult, he or she is stuck with a teenage brain.

ers *have* to smoke. Here are the four main reasons adult smokers would love to quit smoking:

1. Smoking has serious health consequences. On average, each minute of smoking reduces a person's life expectancy by a minute. When you consider that a two-pack-a-day smoker consumes on the order of 600,000 cigarettes in a lifetime, and it takes three to five minutes to smoke a cigarette, this is a significant factor.

2. Smoking is addictive. Once you get hooked it is very difficult to stop. Once hooked, you have to stop every half hour or so and smoke another cigarette. *You have no choice!*

3. Smoking is extremely expensive. Cigarettes range in price from a nickel to a dime each, so if you are consuming 40 a day the cost averages about $1,000 per year. There must be a better way to spend $1,000!

4. Smoking has effects on personal hygiene. Cigarettes are messy and they make your hair, clothes and breath stink.

As a teenager, with a teenager mind, you may think that you are somehow immune to the addictive power of smoking. Somehow you will not become an addict. All you have to do is look at the millions and millions of adult smokers in America today—all of them thought exactly the same thing. You are *no* different.

Offering an Analogy

Another way to understand smoking is to imagine you and I having the following conversation:

Me: Hi, How's it going?

You: Fine.

Me: Hey, I've got this new thing I'd like you to try.

You: Tell me more.

Me: Well, it's a pill I think you will want to start taking.

You: What does this pill do?

Me: First of all, it is a known carcinogen. It is extremely likely you will get lung cancer due to this pill, for example. It is going to cause a lot of other short- and long-term health problems as well. It will make your breath, hair and clothes stink. It will make a mess of your car. You will take this pill about 40 times a day. This pill, by the way, is addictive. Once you start taking it, it will be extremely difficult to stop. And a supply of pills will cost about $2 to $4 a day, depending on where you buy them.

You: I have to pay for this??? Are you kidding??? This pill sounds absolutely disgusting!!! Why in the world would I want to take it???

Me: It will make you think you are cool.

You: Oh, well, why didn't you say so? Sign me up! Where can I get some???

If I offered you a pill like that, would you take it? Yes you would, if you are using your "teenage mind," because being cool is important to you. But look at the price you have to pay. "Being cool" won't matter nearly so much to you once you turn on your adult mind. Plus, smoking isn't nearly as discreet as taking a pill—*everyone* knows that you are a smoker. Unfortunately, for every adult who sees you it's like wearing a big "I'm a Stupid Teenager!" sign around your neck. With a teenager mind you can't see that. In fact, if you are "rebellious" your teenager mind is thinking that is *exactly* what you want to say. However, your adult brain will turn on in a year or two. If you start smoking as a teenager then you are going to be stuck with an addictive habit that is disgusting, expensive, unhealthy and unwanted.

If you are considering smoking, here is something to try: think about waiting until you are 20 to start using cigarettes. They will still be there—cigarettes are *never* going away! See what you think about them at that point. *You will be amazed!*

Why Teenage Girls Are More Vulnerable to Smoking

Mimi Frost and Susan Baxter

In addition to a general desire to be "cool" that causes so many teens to begin smoking, cigarettes have a particular allure for teenage girls. Young women may start smoking to lose weight or as a way to deal with negative emotions. Glamorous images of women smokers in movies and advertising may also affect teenage girls. Mimi Frost and Susan Baxter, writers for the Canadian women's magazine *Chatelaine*, speak with a teen named Terra about why she and her peers are drawn to cigarettes.

B oth boys and girls like the buzz of nicotine, the promise of coolness, the soot of camaraderie. Still, girls have complicated reasons of their own for smoking, according to research published in the *Journal of the American Medical Women's Association*. Primarily, smoking helps girls control their weight, deal with negative emotions, develop an identity and create a mature self-image. "You have to look at the context of their whole lives to understand why girls smoke," says Dawn Hachey, head of Health Canada's tobacco reduction division. Pressures at school, trouble at home or low self-esteem can cause them to light up. And when girls do, they often smoke together—finding sociability in malls or doughnut shops brimming with nicotine and caffeine.

Terra's Story

Sitting in a neighborhood doughnut shop, a flimsy aluminum ashtray before her, 14-year-old Terra has been smoking for three years. A basketball and soccer player, Terra wears a black T-shirt and leather jacket. Her brown hair has been lightened a few shades. In Grade 5, she and her friends used to light butts her parents left in ashtrays: "We all thought it was cool and if we did it we were so much older and more mature . . . we would talk like we were grown-ups and have coffee." For many kids, cigarettes serve as a rite of passage, one deep drag into the grown-up world. Vancouver pediatrician Roger Tonkin, head of the division of adolescent health at the University of British Columbia's department of pediatrics, says, "In the absence of clear social customs, young people in Western society use alcohol and cigarettes as a sign of growing up." Just like Terra, girls typically take up smoking between the ages of 11 and 13. According to Dr. Michele Bloch of the American Medical Women's Association, they want to feel adult faster than boys. And the earlier they start, the more likely they are to get addicted.

> Girls typically take up smoking between the ages of 11 and 13.

Admitting she's addicted, Terra, like many women smokers—and unlike men—sometimes puffs to help deal with negative emotions. And bad moments strike often on the teen threshold. "A couple of weeks ago, I felt fat and ugly. The friends I hang out with are skinny. I just felt bad about myself." So the 120-pound girl stopped eating, smoked constantly and didn't sleep. Worried that Terra might have bulimia or anorexia, friends told

Terra's mother. (Although they probably didn't know it, eating disorders and smoking have been linked by a 1994 French study published in the *International Journal of Eating Disorders*.)

Besides experiencing bad feelings about her body, Terra is starting to notice a difference between how boys and girls are treated. "People say things about you, for instance, a guy can start sleeping around at 13 and he's a stud, but a girl's a slut." Psychologist Carol Gilligan has written that girls Terra's age withdraw as they start to perceive women's still-unequal place in the world. This realization could be another factor in making girls more vulnerable to smoking, says Lorraine Greaves, a London, Ontario, sociologist who studies women and smoking.

> [Cigarette] ads fill women with images of sociability, relaxation and fashionability.

A top-drawer student, Terra feels stupid if she gets a B, yet at the same time, she's been suspended a few times for things such as telling off teachers and laughing at the principal. Terra's coach threatens to throw her off the basketball team if he catches her smoking. She even gets peer pressure from kids who are militant anti-smokers. On top of all that, today's teens must navigate a landscape mined with drugs; besides marijuana, which is commonly diluted with tobacco, high school kids are doing cocaine, ecstasy and acid. "These kids are using cigarettes to cope with difficult lives," says Phyllis Jensen, a Toronto addiction counselor and health researcher who has studied girl smokers and worked with girls in quitting programs. Pointing to family responsibilities and preferential treatment of boys, Jensen says, "Just because they're kids doesn't mean their lives are easy."

Terra's life certainly wasn't easy at the gifted school she left. When she started wearing jewelry and makeup, the other kids— the ones she called nerds—teased her. And along with this more grown-up persona came cigarettes. It seemed like a perfectly reasonable thing to do, because as Richard Pollay, a professor of marketing at the University of British Columbia who specializes in advertising, points out, kids think smoking is more prevalent than it really is.

The Media Glamorize Smoking

The media help make it seem next-door to normal. Cigarettes star in the Guns N' Roses video. Movies cast cigarettes regularly: smoking was featured in *The Client, Who Framed Roger Rabbit* and *The Mask*—which wowed kids with its famous heart-shaped smoke rings. Women smokers on the big screen seem powerful: Sharon Stone in *Basic Instinct,* computer whiz Sandra Bullock in *The Net.* In the past, Hollywood awarded cigarettes plum roles because tobacco companies paid for it. That practice, called product placement, gave cigarettes movie-star glamour.

"It never tasted so good, it's more the way I felt. I loved doing it, it was fun holding the cigarette in my hand—pretending I was all that." Terra would smoke in her room, taking in her reflection, watching her hand, thinking how she blew out the smoke made her look "sophisticated." She says, "I liked the way it looked. That was the main thing." The glamorous grown-up woman Terra saw in her mirror actually reflects back much recent advertising. Teen girls see plenty of U.S. women's magazines—where 7 percent of ads sell tobacco, according to a 1995 report. The Canadian study *Women, Tobacco and the Media* reported that ads fill women with images of sociability, relaxation and fashionability. Advertising expert Pollay says campaigns with funky Joe Camel and Marlboro machismo stress the independence kids crave.

> Like 61 percent of teen smokers, Terra comes from a smoking household.

Canadian teens are no longer immune to such images after the Supreme Court of Canada voted to allow cigarettes on billboards: in fact, last winter, an advertising company placed a billboard for cigarettes directly opposite a school in Hull, Quebec—public outcry quickly brought it down. Plus, in Canada, tobacco companies spend $62 million on sponsorships that get their brands in the public eye. (Like many publications, *Chatelaine* accepts ads for tobacco-sponsored awards and events, believing the benefit outweighs the harm.) Kids are influenced by them. A 20-year study published in the *Journal of Marketing* found teens are three times as likely to respond to cigarette ads as adults.

Terra's Mother

At the doughnut shop, Terra and her mom talk about their smoking. Neither of them lights up, trying to ignore an issue they mostly avoid. Terra's mother, Sandy Pellizzer, 39, started smoking back when cigarettes were everywhere. And like 61 percent of teen smokers, Terra comes from a smoking household. Like many smoking parents, Terra's mother is perturbed that her daughter follows her example: "I don't want your teeth to be yellow, I don't want to hear you cough. I'd like to give you money without thinking where you spend it. I don't want to check up on you to see if you're eating."

Saying that her mother is cool and doesn't hound her, Terra understands her mom's fears. "I think she did all the same things I do. She knows what I'm up to without my telling her anything." In turn, Terra worries about her 12-year-old sister who occasionally gets a buzz from smoking to fit in. "I can't stop her, she sees me doing it all the time." Sandy, a mother of three, imagines that Terra, whose teachers say she could go to any school or get athletic scholarships, will be sucked into the teenage vacuum. Since she works as an assistant manager of a store, Sandy often checks on her daughter at school or at her lunch spot. When the kids see her coming, says Pellizzer, they drop their cigarettes out of respect.

But when Sandy suggests the two of them drop the habit together and make a quitting pact, Terra replies, "I can't imagine you without a cigarette. I don't care if you quit.". . .

Terra's mother . . . hates to think of her daughter smoking and wants the law to help. Several times, Sandy Pellizzer has called police to report local stores that sell cigarettes to minors—but there's no action. It's common across Canada: 60 percent of retailers are willing to sell cigarettes to minors, according to a nationwide compliance check by the Canadian Cancer Society. If police don't enforce the law, it's back in the parents' hands, and Terra's parents don't let her smoke at home.

> We need to understand the issues behind girls' smoking—such as body image, inequality, social needs.

Trying to make her kick the habit, Sandy has cut off Terra's lunch money, to no avail. "Cigarettes are so cheap now," Sandy says. Her daughter actually brags that she can get cigarettes for $2.80 at the local milk store less than what her mother pays.

In her mom's concern, Terra sees hypocrisy. "It's okay for grown-ups but not for kids. It shouldn't be that way. You should be stressing it for everybody. Then, maybe the kids would think, 'It's not good for them, it's not good for me.'"

Suggested Policies

That contradiction remains a part of the problem. "The policies don't back up our educational message," says Heather Selin, a policy analyst for the Non-Smokers' Rights Association, the antitobacco lobby group. Cigarettes sell for three bucks a pack, whereas nicotine patches cost about $75. In the same month Health Canada announced its $104 million tobacco-reduction plan, the government lowered cigarette taxes. "Regulation must accompany education," says Selin.

If mothers can't persuade their daughters not to smoke, what can? No single solution will do; smoking needs to be attacked on all fronts. "Looking at it as simply a health problem won't work," says sociologist Lorraine Greaves, author of *Smoke Screen: Women's Smoking and Social Control*. Greaves says we need to understand the issues behind girls' smoking—such as body image, inequality, social needs—and address them as well. As more and more girls smoke, Health Canada has finally responded by creating an initiative on women and tobacco. In 1996, it [unveiled] three special programs developed especially for girls—which teach media literacy, promote sport and teach coping skills. Although new, they're a move in the right direction. So are antismoking policies with real teeth that bite.

Explaining the Rise in Smoking Among African-American Teenagers

Phillip Gardiner

African-American youth smoke less than any other group of teenagers. However, the percentage of African-American teens that smoke almost doubled between 1991 and 1997. According to Phillip Gardiner, this sharp increase has several factors, including advertising that targets African Americans and the use of nicotine to intensify a marijuana high. Gardiner is a research administrator at the Tobacco-Related Disease Research program, which supports research on how to prevent and treat tobacco-related diseases.

Researchers, health educators, and parents were rudely awakened on April 3, 1998, when the Centers for Disease Control and Prevention (CDC) reported that African American youth smoking rates had increased sharply from 12.6% to 22.7%, an 80% increase from 1991 to 1997. As if to add insult to injury, the most recent *Report of the Surgeon General: To-*

Reprinted from Phillip Gardiner, "Increases in African American Tobacco Use Pose New Challenges," *Tobacco-Related Disease Research Program Newsletter*, July 1998. Reprinted with permission from the author.

bacco Use Among U.S. Racial/Ethnic Minority Groups not only confirmed the CDC findings from earlier in the month, but went even further, stating that African American men stand the greatest risk of dying from lung cancer. 81% of African American men who smoke and have contracted lung cancer die from the disease, compared with 54% of their white counterparts. In short, smoking and tobacco use in the African American community is a growing and deadly public health issue that must be addressed by tobacco researchers.

Tobacco use (including cigarettes, cigars, and smokeless tobacco) increased among all teenagers in the 1990s. Tobacco use was highest among non-Hispanic white students, with more than 50% of white males saying they had used some form of tobacco in the preceding month. Cigarette smoking was also most prevalent among white students: 39.7% percent reported cigarette use, an increase from 30.9% in 1991. Over 33% of Hispanic students smoked cigarettes and 50% of American Indians youth reported smoking cigarettes. Yet, the increases were most striking among young black males, whose low cigarette smoking rates were once deemed a public health success story. In 1991, 14.1% of Black male high school students smoked cigarettes, but by 1997, twice as many youth reported (28.2%) smoking cigarettes. While African American teenage girls' smoking rates also rose (11.3%–17.4%), their rate actually dropped in the years 1993–1995.

> Smoking and tobacco use in the African American community is a growing and deadly public health issue.

Why Smoking Among African Americans Has Increased

A host of factors have been identified as contributing to the increases in African American smoking: the glamorization of tobacco products, especially cigars, in the movies and on television; the relatively stable price of cigarettes in the 1990's; and the tobacco industry marketing directly to African Americans. The release of tobacco industry documents confirms years of suspicion that tobacco companies have especially targeted African Americans. Documents show that as early as the 1960's, the motivations of the "negro" tobacco consumer were a major concern of R.J. Reynolds. Moreover, other documentation confirm that R.J. Reynolds, which makes Salems, and Brown & Williamson, which makes Kools, were constantly contending for the African American mentholated cigarette market. One of the more conspicuous expressions of targeted marketing is the Kool Jazz Festival, which annually travels the country promoting cigarette smoking and attracting large numbers of African Americans.

> An increase in tobacco use among young African Americans has also been linked to marijuana use.

The impact of years of targeted advertising is seen in the brand loyalty of African American teenagers. Generally speaking, Marlboro and Camel portray white images and characters and are the brands of choice among white teens. On the other hand, Kool and Newport use black and other minority images and are favored by African American teens. Additionally, we know from previous research that teens mimic their parents in their smoking habits; white adults smoke Marlboro and Camels, African American adults smoke mentholated brands.

Marijuana and Tobacco

An increase in tobacco use among young African Americans has also been linked to marijuana use. Robin Mermelstein, Ph.D., University of Illinois at Chicago, speaking of the findings from focus groups held among 1,200 teenagers, points out that many black teens were drawn to cigarettes because nicotine intensifies their marijuana high. Similarly, Charyn Sutton, who works for a

Philadelphia marketing company, calls the phenomenon the "reverse gateway effect." Traditionally, white youth have proceeded from legal substances to illegal substances. Here we have findings that show that some black teens are taking the opposite path. In addition, some young African Americans empty out the insides of cigars and refill them with marijuana and/or crack cocaine among other substances. These concoctions called variously "Philly Blunts" or sometimes "Caviar" have augmented cigar and tobacco use among teenage blacks. It is important to note that while crack cocaine use has declined, marijuana and, increasingly, tobacco use appears to be rampant among African American youth.

The rise in African American teen tobacco smoking coupled with marijuana usage presents new challenges and thorny questions that tobacco control experts and nicotine addiction researchers must grapple with. Scientists know that tetrahydrocannabinol (THC), the active ingredient in marijuana, and nicotine both influence the dopaminergic pathway, which is involved in the neural reward mechanism. Is it possible there is a synergistic effect of these two drugs on brain chemistry? Does the combined use of tobacco and marijuana produce greater neuropharmacological effects than if the two drugs are used separately? Does THC extend the addictive qualities of nicotine?

Conflicting Statistics

Surprisingly, a current California Tobacco Control Section (TCS) survey depicts a much different picture of African American teenage smoking rates than that seen nationally. According to TCS, African American teen smoking has dropped from 6% in 1992 to 3.6% in 1997. This nearly 50% decrease is in striking contrast to the 80% increase in African American smoking rates reported nationally. Interestingly, TCS figures show increases in white and Hispanic teen smoking during the 1990's. White teen smoking increased from 10.3% in 1992 to 12.5% in 1997. Similarly, Hispanic teen smoking increased from 7.8% in 1992 to 11.9% in 1997.

Tobacco researchers must ask why smoking among California African Americans is in decline when national rates are up. While tobacco control efforts have been important in the California Black community, the question is begged: are there other contributing factors? Other researchers might ask whether the TCS figures are replicable.

> Not only hasn't smoking been controlled, it is actually growing among young people, especially African American youth.

Behavioral scientists are faced with still other questions. Why do white youth typically proceed from tobacco to marijuana while many black youth proceed from marijuana to tobacco? Has the cigar smoking craze, promoted by the tobacco industry and Hollywood, exacerbated "Philly Blunt" use among African American teens? Even though African American teen smoking rates have escalated nationally in the past 8 years, the prevalence in this population is still the lowest compared to other ethnic groups. What are the factors that have so far protected African American youth from higher rates of smoking? Moreover, what are the factors that lead African American youth from the lowest rates of smoking to become African American adults with the highest rates of smoking? What is it that takes place during the years 18–24 that increases cigarette smoking among this population?

The CDC report, the most recent Report of the Surgeon General and other research reported in this article should serve as a wake up call for tobacco researchers. Not only hasn't smoking been controlled, it is actually growing among young people, especially African American youth, one of the most vulnerable sectors of the population.

Point of Contention: Does Advertising Encourage Teens to Smoke?

Antismoking organizations have long targeted advertising as a key factor in teen smoking. Their argument was bolstered in 1998 by a study published in the *Journal of the American Medical Association*, which concluded that approximately one-third of the adolescents who experiment with tobacco do so because of promotional advertising. In November 1998, as the tobacco industry faced a class-action lawsuit that it knowingly sold dangerous products, the industry agreed to a $206 billion settlement. This settlement placed restrictions on how tobacco could be marketed—companies could not target youths in their advertising or sponsor sports events with underage participants, for example. Despite the study and settlement, disagreement persists as to the impact advertising has on teenagers' decision to smoke. *America*, a weekly Catholic magazine of opinion on social, political, and religious issues, argues that tobacco ads and promotions entice children and teenagers to smoke, and thus should be banned, while Jacob Sullum, a senior editor at *Reason* magazine, asserts that studies linking advertising to smoking are poorly constructed and inaccurate.

Advertising Encourages Teens to Smoke

America

"Got a light?" Older Americans might associate this question with sophisticated adults in a movie from the 1940's or 1950's. Nowadays, however, it is frequently being asked by children under 18. Health officials estimate that each day 3,000 children start smoking, most of them between the ages of 10 and 18; they account for 90 percent of all new smokers. A third will die of smoking-related diseases.

New Regulations

In an effort to curb tobacco use among youth, the Department of Health and Human Services issued regulations in January 1996, aimed at enforcing the ban on selling tobacco to anyone under 18 by penalizing states that do not monitor tobacco sales in stores. But the very fact that the tobacco industry supports the new regulations suggests they may lack teeth. Health advocates and anti-smoking groups contend that far more is needed, notably proposals made by the Food and Drug Administration in July 1995. At that time the F.D.A. urged that nicotine be classified as an addictive drug, that cigarette vending machines be banned (a major source of tobacco for the underaged) and that advertising aimed at youth be restricted.

In August 1995 President Clinton, to his credit, supported the F.D.A. proposals and expressed his hope that smoking by children and teen-agers could be reduced by 50 percent within seven years after the proposals receive congressional approval. But the F.D.A.'s desire to classify nicotine as an addictive drug is sure to be fiercely resisted by the tobacco industry, as will restrictions on advertising. Resistance can also be expected from members of Congress representing tobacco growing states, as well as from those who receive substantial contributions from the industry. In the first half of 1995, the industry donated $1.5 million to the Republican Party treasury, a 400 percent increase over the previous year's contribution in the same period.

Targeting Youth

Especially disturbing to child health advocates is advertising that targets youth. A study described in the *Journal of the American Medical Association* (12/11/91) noted that among children of kindergarten age, R.J. Reynolds's cartoon character, Joe Camel, is as familiar as the Mickey Mouse logo of the Disney television channel. Two other studies released in October and November of 1995—one reported in the *Journal of the National Cancer Institute*, the other in *Health Psychology*—found that children receptive to advertising are two to four times as likely to begin smoking as those who are not and that there is a correlation between promotional campaigns with free T-shirts and the like and smoking among children aged 14 to 17.

The industry denies targeting people under 21 and claims that its advertising goal is simply to promote brand switching and brand loyalty. But it is well aware that children and teens do not have the

> Children receptive to advertising are two to four times as likely to begin smoking as those who are not.

experience and information to weigh the dangers of smoking. That is why they represent what one anti-smoking advocate, Representative Henry A. Waxman, Democrat of California, has called a tobacco advertiser's dream. An internal R.J. Reynolds memo obtained and described by the *Washington Post* (10/14/95) shows that as early as 1973 the youth market was being kept in careful focus. The memo outlines a strategy for attracting what it calls "learning smokers." Scott Ballin, chairman of the Coalition on Smoking OR Health—composed of the American Cancer Society, the American Lung Association and the American Heart Association—described the memo as clear evidence of youth targeting.

Pregnant teens and young women are at particular risk because of the danger to their unborn children. Smoking during pregnancy is linked with increased risk of infant mortality and low birth weight. William J. Cox, executive director of the Catholic Health Association, described this aspect of the situation as a pro-life matter: "The pro-life community is committed to protecting not only the life of the unborn child, but its health as well."

Mr. Cox also noted that young women in their teens represent the largest group of new smokers. This may be the result, at least in part, of the barrage of advertising specifically directed toward them since the late 1960's. Ad campaigns like that of Philip Morris for its highly successful Virginia Slims brand, using the slogan "You've Come a Long Way, Baby," have been associated with sudden increases in smoking by girls 11 to 17 years old. The appeal of such ads, with their use of magic words like "slim," is especially strong for those who may be self-conscious about their weight.

For these and other young women who become addicted and continue smoking, the price in terms of mortality is high. As a direct result of increased tobacco use, lung cancer now surpasses breast cancer as the number one cause of cancer deaths among women. The tobacco industry is well aware of facts like these but places concern for profit above considerations of public health. After all, if children and teen-agers did not begin smoking, the industry's sales in this country would shrivel up—and more Americans would not have their lives cut short. A telling cartoon in the *Philadelphia Inquirer* shows an industry representative saying: "Hardly anyone over 21 starts smoking. We don't *want* to target your kids. We have no choice." In the final panel of the cartoon we see the representative standing by a crib; in it, a baby reaches up toward toys suspended from a mobile above in the shape of cigarette packs and, yes, the head of Joe Camel.

Advertising Does Not Cause Teenagers to Smoke

Jacob Sullum

If Congress approves tobacco legislation this year, it will be part of a deal that dramatically changes the way cigarette companies promote their products: no more outdoor ads, human or cartoon figures, sporting event sponsorships, trinkets or clothing embossed with brand names, or ads in magazines that teenagers like to read. Not content to wait, cities across the country are imposing their own limits on cigarette signs and billboards.

Evaluating a Study
The premise behind these restrictions is that fewer ads will

mean fewer smokers. Yet there is remarkably little evidence that advertising plays an important role in getting people to smoke, as opposed to getting them to smoke a particular brand. Every time a study purports to show that people smoke because of advertising and promotion, a close examination reveals that it actually shows something else.

> There is remarkably little evidence that advertising plays an important role in getting people to smoke.

[One] example is a study reported in the February 18, 1998, *Journal of the American Medical Association*. The authors, led by University of California at San Diego researcher John P. Pierce, claimed to be presenting "the first longitudinal evidence . . . that tobacco promotional activities are causally related to the onset of smoking." They estimated that one-third of adolescent experimentation with cigarettes, involving 700,000 American teenagers each year, "can be attributed to tobacco promotional activities."

As usual, newspapers uncritically regurgitated the researchers' conclusions. "Advertising, Teen Smoking Found Related," said the headline in the *San Diego Union-Tribune*. The article quoted Pierce as saying, "Our study is the first to conclusively prove that the effect of tobacco marketing happens at the very beginning, and encourages teens to start the process of becoming a smoker."

According to the *Washington Post*, Pierce et al.'s findings "indicate that young people's decisions to begin smoking are influenced by advertising." The *New York Times* said the study "concluded that exposure to cigarette advertising was a significant factor in whether teen-agers took up smoking."

Asking the Wrong Questions

In reality, the study did not even measure "exposure to cigarette advertising." Instead, Pierce and his colleagues surveyed California teenagers and assessed their "receptivity to tobacco advertising and promotional activities" by asking them about the cigarette brand they had seen advertised most often, their favorite cigarette ad, and their use or willingness to use a cigarette promotional item (such as a jacket or flashlight). They also asked the teenagers whether they smoked and, if not, whether they might in the future.

Three years later, the researchers re-interviewed 1,752 of the respondents who had said they didn't smoke and didn't think they would. The more "receptive" ones were more likely to have "progressed toward smoking," meaning they now said they might smoke, reported experimenting with cigarettes, or had smoked a total of five packs or more.

Of the teenagers who had said they owned or might obtain a promotional item (classified as highly receptive), 62 percent had moved in the direction of smoking, compared to 38 percent of those who couldn't name the most advertised brand and said they weren't willing to own a promotional item (classified as minimally receptive). Only 22 percent of the minimally receptive teenagers had experimented with cigarettes, compared to 34 percent of the others. Based on the difference between those two rates, Pierce et al. blamed one-third of experimentation on advertising and promotion.

The problem is, the researchers never measured exposure to this evil influence, let alone showed that it was correlated with smoking. So far as we know, all of these teenagers, whether they had started smoking or not, were exposed to the same amount of advertising and promotion.

The variable that Pierce et al. did measure, "receptivity," seems to be a pretty good index of attitudes toward smoking. It stands to reason that teenagers who strongly disapprove of the habit are less likely to smoke and also less likely to admire a Camel ad or own a Marlboro tote bag. And it's hardly surprising that teenagers who express a positive attitude toward such things are more likely to try cigarettes at some point, even if they once told an interviewer they had no interest in smoking.

Pierce and his colleagues were so determined to indict advertising and promotion that they never addressed the question of what makes some teenagers more "receptive" than others. Neither did any of the press reports I saw Which suggests another hypothesis: Perhaps receptivity to politically correct beliefs is associated with progression toward scientifically shaky conclusions.

Jacob Sullum, "Bad Influence," *Reason Online,* February 25, 1998. http://reason.com/sullum/022598.html.

Chapter 2

Perspectives on Teen Smoking

Four Teens Share Their Views

Brandi Battle, Kellie Jolly, Nickita Bradley, and Josh

Four young adults—Brandi Battle, Kellie Jolly, Nickita Bradley, and Josh—offer testimony on how they decided whether to smoke. Brandi says she decided not to smoke due to health and religious reasons. Kellie points to her involvement in athletics as her main reason not to smoke. Nickita testifies that she used to smoke but stopped after learning she was pregnant. Josh, the only smoker of the four, says he started because of peer pressure and continues to smoke despite his parents' protests. The teens testified before a 1997 Senate committee hearing titled "Public Forum on Youth and Tobacco: Breaking the Cycle."

Senator Bill Frist: Despite the great public outcry in this country against smoking, particularly against teen smoking, we have not even begun to apply all at our public health and private resources, especially at the community level. I am grateful for the attention this issue is receiving and look forward to the interaction that we will have [at this hearing]. . . .

Let me turn to the first panel. Brandi is a 14-year-old from Washington, DC, who will be sharing with us how her church

Excerpted from Brandi Battle, Kellie Jolly, Nickita Bradley, and Josh, "Public Forum on Youth and Tobacco: Breaking the Cycle," congressional testimony before the Senate Subcommittee on Public Health and Safety, October 27, 1997.

youth group, the Youth for Christ from the Anacostia Gospel Church, has influenced her decision about whether to smoke. This church's outstanding work in the DC inner city has been prominently featured in the media.

Kellie from Sparta, Tennessee, is a 20-year-old member of the national champion women's basketball team at the University of Tennessee. She will be talking to us about how participation in athletics steers teens away from smoking.

> "Some people start smoking because they are looking for acceptance from their peers."

Nickita is an 18-year-old from Maryland who began smoking at age 14 but stopped 2 years later. She will be relating how her experience with pregnancy and motherhood affected her decision to quit.

Finally, we will hear from Josh, who is 16-years-old. Josh is a current smoker whose story will help us better understand the factors behind youth smoking.

With that, I will turn to Brandi and we will move straight down the line. Brandi, welcome, and thank you for being with us today.

Brandi's Story

Ms. Battle: Good afternoon. My name is Brandi Battle. I am 14-years-old and I am in the ninth grade at Patricia Roberts Harris Educational Center in Southeast Washington, DC. I am speaking to you today on behalf of myself and the youth at Anacostia Gospel Chapel.

As you know, smoking is very hazardous to your health. Smoking can make you very sick. It can cause cancer. I once saw a picture in science class of two lungs, one of a smoker and one of a nonsmoker. The visual comparison was astonishing. One lung of the smoker was as black as tar. One lung of the non-smoker was pink and perfectly normal. This shows how harmful smoking is and how it can shorten your life.

Some people start smoking because they are looking for acceptance from their peers. Other kids smoke because they watch their parents smoke, so they follow their parents' examples. My mother smoked and her father smoked, too. Many of my relatives smoke on both sides of the family. It seems natural that I would start smoking, also.

However, I have made a commitment not to smoke for many reasons. As the daughter of a smoker, I know that smoking affects not only the smokers but also those who live with them. The smell of smoke gets in everything, the air, clothing, and hair. Victims of fire often die from smoke inhalation, but I live with it every day. As an athlete, I need to keep a strong and healthy body. Smoking will prevent me from doing my very best. I have never personally seen anyone die from smoking, but each day, I watch my mother smoke herself into an early grave.

As an educated black woman, I do not wish to begin an expensive, addictive habit that will give me

> "By playing sports, I think athletes are more likely to refrain from smoking."

bad breath, stained teeth, irritated eyes, headaches, and shortness of breath. As a young woman of faith, I will not start smoking because I want to obey God's word. I do not wish to defile his temple, which is my body. I am too smart to begin a lifestyle that is self-destructive. Some people may get pleasure and satisfaction from smoking. My satisfaction comes not from smoking but from the personal relationship with Jesus Christ.

Senator Frist: Brandi, thank you.

Sports and Smoking

Ms. Jolly: Thank you, Senator. I personally have grown up in a nonsmoking home and, therefore, I have not been subject to smokers, but I have never considered smoking. I have more of a reason not to smoke because I am an athlete. I have to take precautions to keep myself healthy so that I can reach my peak performance. Basketball has provided me with many opportunities, and I must stay healthy to reach my goals.

I know that even a light smoker can feel respiratory strain and a reduction in performance. As my trainer has passed along to me, I know that carbon monoxide, which is a component in smoke, limits the oxygen carried into the blood stream. Therefore, maximum exercise capacity is lowered.

Nicotine increases the resistance of air flow in and out of the lungs by constricting the airways. Smoking also paralyzes the scilla in the lungs, and the scilla is responsible for clearing and removing debris in from the lungs. Therefore, the debris is accumulated when the scilla is not functioning

By playing sports, I think athletes are more likely to refrain from smoking and I think that athletes are going to do what is best for their bodies and I do not think it should be any different from anyone else.

Senator Frist: Thank you, Kellie.

A Teenage Mother

Ms. Bradley: Good afternoon, Mr. Chairman. My name is Nickita Bradley and with me is my son, Patrick. I am 18-years-old and live in Baltimore City.

Like so many other teens in my community, I began smoking when I was 14-years-old. At that time, because of pressure from my friends and family and other things happening in my life, smoking seemed to be the thing to do. Two years later, I was still smoking and found out that I was pregnant. I continued to smoke during the first 2 months of my pregnancy and then I quit. It was very hard to stop smoking. I tried the patch and the gum, but none seemed to work, but then I just quit "cold turkey".

Let me tell you why I quit. My mother has been a smoker most of her life, and although I feel healthy, I do have asthma. It is not clear to me whether my mother's smoking contributed to this or not, but enough. I have an older brother named Marquis who was a premature, low birth weight baby. Today, he still has certain disabilities in his life. We will never know what effects my mother's smoking had on his health problems.

> "There is a lot of pressure put on teens from their friends to join the crowd and become a smoker."

Based on this experience, I was determined to do everything I could to give birth to a healthy baby. I owed it to my baby to stop smoking, and I am proud to say that Patrick weighed eight pounds, nine ounces at birth and is still healthy.

Smoking is a terrible habit. It messes with your health, but there is a lot of pressure put on teens from their friends to join the crowd and become a smoker.

Let me finish by telling you what the Baltimore City Healthy Start Program means to me. It is a great program that helps build character. It shows women and teens how to be a caring mother. Healthy Start helped me with setting goals for my future. I just finished my GED [General Education Development] diploma classes at Healthy Start Center. Also, I am looking forward to going to school to be a culinary artist in the near future.

As a nonsmoker and a current mother, my life is on the right track. Thank you so much.

Senator Frist: Thank you, Nickita.

A Current Smoker Speaks

Josh: Good afternoon. My name is Josh and I live in Virginia. I am 16-years-old and I am in the 11th grade.

My first experience with smoking was when I was about 9-years-old. My little brother and I were wondering what it was like to smoke, so we got one of my dad's packs of cigarettes and brought it in the backyard and tried to smoke. We did not know how, so we could not get it lit. We were trying to blow out instead of drawing in. My dad found out and he made me sit inside and smoke several cigarettes in thinking this would prevent me from wanting to smoke anymore. I felt really sick that night, and so for a long time, I did not even go near cigarettes.

The next experience I had was when I was with one of my friends. He had gotten a pack of cigarettes, and so we went into his backyard and smoked a few. It was not really fun or anything. I was just smoking because of the whole peer pressure thing. But every once in a while when we got together, we had one. We would go around the corner or whatever and smoke a cigarette. I stopped when I stopped hanging out with him about four or five months later.

Tobacco Use, Grades 6–12

	White	Black	Hispanic	Total
Cigarettes				
Middle	8.8%	9.0%	11.0%	9.2%
High	32.8	15.8	25.8	28.4
Cigars				
Middle	4.9	8.8	7.6	6.1
High	16.0	14.8	13.4	15.3
Bidis (Indian)				
Middle	1.8	2.8	3.5	2.4
High	4.4	5.8	5.6	5.0
Kreteks (Indonesian clove-flavored)				
Middle	1.7	1.7	2.1	1.9
High	6.5	2.8	5.5	5.8

Using any tobacco products*

Middle school students

White	Black	Hispanic	Total
11.6%	14.4%	15.2%	12.8%

High school students

White	Black	Hispanic	Total
39.4%	24.0%	30.7%	34.8%

*Includes pipes and smokeless tobacco, in addition to the forms listed.

Centers for Disease Control and Prevention

After that, I did not really smoke for about a year, until I was about 12. How I got started was one day when I was outside, I found one of my dad's cigarette butts that had not had much smoked off of it. I was interested in trying it out again, so I brought it into the backyard and smoked it. I got a buzz and thought it was cool, so from then on, I would look for half-smoked cigarettes to smoke. I did not know why. They taste pretty bad.

But then I started sneaking packs from my dad. Sometimes he

would notice and ask me and my brother about it. I would deny anything about it and he would believe me. I got to where I was smoking pretty regularly. Sometimes my parents would pick up on it, smelling it on me. I got in trouble when they smelled it on me, so I had to be pretty careful about it.

Then I started meeting people and found out how to get cigarettes, and from then on, I smoked Camels. I was smoking about half a pack a day and I was always in trouble with my parents about it and getting grounded for it. This went on for a long time. Finally, they pretty much got tired of the constant conflict and just let me smoke. They figured I was just going to do it anyway and I had not listened to them over the past year. So I continued to smoke and just did not let them see me smoking and it was just left at that. My parents were worried about me asking strangers to buy me cigarettes, so they started buying them for me with my money.

Right now, I smoke from a half a pack a day to one pack. I have tried to quit a couple of times using the patch and nicotine gum because my parents were really getting on me about trying to quit. So I gave it a try, but it did not work. I guess I did not really want to quit. It is more of a mental thing than a physical thing. I crave the actual physical part of smoking, inhaling it and having it in my hand, plus a lot of my friends smoke. I am sure I will want to quit sometime, I am just not sure when.

Questions About Smoking

Senator Frist: Josh, thank you very much.

I thank all of you for your comments, and what I would like to do is spend a few minutes among all of us and just have a discussion and bring out some of the points that many of you have mentioned, and the range is really wonderful. This is the most important panel today. If we do our job as policy makers, our job is to reduce and ultimately eliminate teen smoking, so I want to thank all of you for taking time to come and share your thoughts and your feelings and attitudes with us.

Brandi, I want to begin by saying what a great example you are for people all across America. Your family and your friends must be very proud of you. I do want to ask you a little bit about the pressures that you must resist day in, day out, not to smoke, against smoking. Do many of your friends smoke right now?

Ms. Battle: No.

Senator Frist: So one out of ten, or one out of five, or—

Ms. Battle: Out of five.

Senator Frist: One out of five. Why do you think more of them do not smoke?

Ms. Battle: They are not around people who smoke all the time. They are just their own person.

Senator Frist: And then right now, are you ever pressured day in, day out, to smoke? Do people come up and say, "Brandi, why are you not smoking? We are out smoking." Do you feel that pressure at all?

Ms. Battle: No.

The Influence of Advertising

Senator Frist: Let me ask you, Brandi, and then, Josh, maybe you, as well, about advertising. It is something that we talk about in these rooms day in, day out, the importance of advertising, the importance of Joe Camel, the importance of billboards. Josh, let me ask you, do you feel any pressures to smoke or not to smoke, and also I am thinking of your friends, as well. You said that you have tried to stop smoking, that you do smoke, and will try to stop again in the future probably at some point. What is the role of advertising, the billboards, and what do your friends say about it?

> "I crave the actual physical part of smoking, inhaling it and having it in my hand."

Josh: Most of the advertising that I have gotten is from, like, looking at magazines and stuff, but I do not really talk much about my friends, why they—what brand they picked and stuff. Right now, I am smoking Newports just because all my friends do smoke Newports. I do not know. The reason why I picked Camels was it appealed to me at the time and it had the "Camel cash" on the back and I thought that was cool, but—

> "I know that when I was in high school, the people that did smoke were the people that had nothing to do after school."

Senator Frist: And Brandi, what about you? When you see those billboards and the magazines and the advertising, again, answer for yourself but also your friends, what is your impression in terms of the importance of that advertising?

Ms. Battle: I do not feel any pressure because I just see what it does to other people and my mother, and my friends are basically my age, so they do not really think about smoking. They just think about what they can wear to school and mostly just doing their work, I guess.

Senator Frist: Nickita, how would you answer that in terms of the advertising and billboards and magazines? Do you think that influences people your age to start smoking?

Ms. Bradley: I feel as though it does very much that. As for myself, I do not take notice to the billboards. I feel as though it is just another opportunity to get people to smoke, but I feel also that I never paid any notice to it.

Community Involvement

Senator Frist: Kellie, clearly, being in athletics, you found it to be an environment in which smoking is not encouraged and where there is clearly a detrimental effect to your performance if you did smoke. Do you have many friends who smoke? Obviously, you spend a lot of time with basketball, but outside of that?

Ms. Jolly: No. I do not have any close friends that smoke.

Senator Frist: Have you ever smoked?

Ms. Jolly: I have never smoked in my life.

Senator Frist: Are there community efforts? I think it is unusual. Again, sports puts you in that sort of environment. Is there anything going on in your community that would either encourage or discourage people from smoking, or is it predominately athletics?

Ms. Jolly: I think that community, involving youths, I think where I am from, athletics is a big part of what youths do and, therefore, it keeps them busy with something else and they are not getting pressured from friends to smoke. I know that when I was in high school, the people that did smoke were the people that had nothing to do after school, that were not involved with extracurricular activities, and whose family background were smokers.

Senator Frist: Thank you.

Regrets of Teen Smokers

Patricia J. Murphy

In the following article, Patricia J. Murphy presents the stories of two teenage smokers who regret having started smoking and have either quit or are trying to do so. Sean started smoking as a way to fit in among older kids and to feel better about himself. He smoked for five years, and also became addicted to drugs and alcohol, before quitting. Laura began smoking out of curiosity and because she felt rebellious, and now wants to quit because of the health risks. She has yet to succeed, although she has reduced the number of cigarettes she smokes. Both teenagers say they regret the money and time they wasted on cigarettes and wish they had never started. Murphy is a writer for the magazine *Current Health*.

As many as 3,000 American teens begin smoking each day. One-third will die from tobacco-related deaths. If smoking doesn't kill you, it'll yellow your teeth and fingernails; dull your senses; make you cough; give you frequent colds, chronic bronchitis, gastric ulcers, and bad circulation; increase your heart rate and blood pressure; wrinkle your skin—and reduce your

Reprinted from Patricia J. Murphy, "Teen Smokers Tell Their Tale," *Current Health*, November 1999, vol. 26, no. 3. Published and copyrighted by Weekly Reader Corporation. All rights reserved.

life span. So, why would anyone start?

Two teens who did, Sean and Laura, share their stories in the hope you won't become an addicted smoker like them.

Sean's Story

Sean, 17, lives in Buffalo Grove, Illinois. He started smoking when he was 12 years old "to fit in" with the older crowd he ran around with. "I remember my first time smoking," says Sean. "I liked fitting in with the older kids, but I didn't feel so good." But soon after, Sean felt the need to light up—to relax and escape from his everyday life. These feelings came from the nicotine in tobacco.

Because nicotine's a powerful addictive drug, it affects both the brain and the nervous system and can stimulate nerve cells, making the smoker feel either anxious or relaxed. First-time smokers' ex-

> Tobacco often can be more addictive than cocaine, heroin, or marijuana.

periences may be unpleasant like Sean's cough, dizziness, and nausea. But, with repeated use, most people experience increased tolerance and dependence. That means that with each puff, Sean and others become used to a certain amount of nicotine in the blood-stream, so they need more to feel the same effect. Increased tolerance and dependence on nicotine are why smokers often go from a few cigarettes a day to a pack—or more!

Because of repeated exposure to nicotine, smokers become physically and psychologically addicted. Tobacco often can be more addictive than cocaine, heroin, or marijuana, according to the American Cancer Society. Some experts believe tobacco to be a "gateway" drug that can lead smokers to other drugs. Sean agrees.

"Smoking begins as a 'social thing' until you become addicted," says Sean. "Then, once you're addicted, it's up to you. The group that I smoked with wasn't a 'good' group. They experimented with a lot of things, including drugs. Hanging out with them was like throwing dice. I made a wrong move." Sean became addicted to drugs and alcohol.

The move landed him in drug/alcohol rehabilitation. There, he was able to quit drugs and alcohol but was unable to kick his smoking habit.

A Helpful Program

In order to fight his addiction and stop his smoking [in fall 1999], Sean enrolled in SOS—Stop Our Smoking, a voluntary, seven-week smoking-cessation program at his school, Stevenson High School. Kathy White, designer and facilitator of the program, says that it motivates teens to understand their habit, to learn about the addiction, to identify coping skills, stress management, and nutrition and exercise techniques—and to stop smoking.

"We talk about the physical addiction that comes with smoking—the craving—the way the body itches to satisfy itself with a cigarette— and the psychological addiction. How it comforts, distracts, decreases stress—and how cigarettes become a best friend," says White.

SOS tries to ruin this deadly friendship. "The teens work diligently on problem-solving and choosing alternative behaviors to stop incidences of smoking. Talking helps, so does deep breathing, carrying a straw to chew on, or wearing a rubber band around your wrist and snapping it when you feel an urge to smoke," says White.

> The earlier teens start smoking, the worse the damage can be to their developing lungs.

It worked for Sean. "In SOS, something just clicked. I started caring about my body, my diet—and I started weight training," says Sean. "SOS taught me the benefits of quitting, had me list the pros and cons. The pros outweighed the cons, so I threw my cigarettes out the window and quit."

Sean began using behaviors he learned through SOS to help him remain smoke-free. He started focusing on boxing and eating to gain weight. And he's trying out for his high school's football team. "I've spent three years in high school, and only one year did I go out for a sport. But I didn't stick with it. I couldn't take the practices because I didn't have the lungs for it," says Sean.

Now, Sean has the lungs for anything. Being smoke-free, he's running and working out every day and feeling great. Looking back on his smoke-filled days, he realizes the toll it took on his body—and his wallet.

"Outside of the health risks, it's ridiculous—the amount of money I blew smoking. I've done the math. I could have taken a helicopter to school every day with the money I spent on cigarettes," says Sean.

Laura's Story

Laura, 17, of Vernon Hills, Illinois, began smoking with her friends four years ago at the age of 13, out of curiosity and what she calls a "rebellious urge."

Today, she still fights the urge for a cigarette. She has tried to quit smoking two other times, but this time she is refusing to let her addiction win. With the help of family and friends and the SOS program at her high school, she's down from a pack to six cigarettes a day and wants to quit before her 18th birthday.

"I started to smoke because I thought everyone was doing it, and I wanted to be able to do it, too," says Laura. "Then, it was something to do; I guess I was bored. At first, I liked it. It seemed to calm me down, but then I got addicted. I should have quit before then."

That was before she developed the smoker's cough, the wheezing in her lungs, and the smell of the smoke in her hair, her clothes, her breath. After four years of smoking, she's worried about the health risks.

Besides an increased risk of disease (cancer, emphysema, and heart disease), teen smokers are at a greater risk than adult smokers of damaging the DNA in their lungs. Moreover, according to a study from University of California at San Francisco School of Medicine, the earlier teens start smoking, the worse the damage can be to their developing lungs.

"Kids think they're invincible. They're not," says Dr. John Minna, a lung cancer expert and director of the Hamon Center of Cancer at the University of Texas Southwestern Medical Center in Dallas, Texas. "We've got to figure out how to get them not to smoke those first cigarettes."

Trying to Cut Down

For now, Laura has figured out how to cut down the number of cigarettes she smokes. She has replaced cigarettes with bottled water and avoids hanging out with friends when they're smoking. She admits that smoke-filled parties are the hardest part of quitting, but her boyfriend (an ex-smoker) offers her encouragement.

"He doesn't pressure me to quit but supports me. He'd like me to live a long time. Sometimes, when I smoke around him, I feel like an idiot."

Laura also feels the positive health effects of cutting back on cigarettes. "I know that I'm giving up some of the nasty stuff (tar, nicotine, etc.) and getting it out of my system."

She looks forward to a time when she'll enjoy the rest of the health benefits of being smoke-free. According to the American Cancer Society, Laura can expect to experience normal blood pressure, pulse, and temperature in her hands and feet within an hour of quitting. Within a day, she'll increase the oxygen and decrease the carbon monoxide levels in her blood, reducing the risk of having a heart attack. Within weeks, she'll begin to breathe easier, her sense of taste and smell will return, and she'll be completely free of nicotine. After 10 years, her risk of lung cancer will be reduced.

> [A smoker] can expect to experience normal blood pressure, pulse, and temperature in her hands and feet within an hour of quitting.

In the meantime, Laura will reduce her cigarettes to four in the coming week, two the following, and none the third. Whenever she feels uptight or has a "nic fit" (need for nicotine), she works out and weight trains. She says that she needs the strength to quit this last and final time.

"I wish I'd never started," says Laura. "It's not worth the time, the money, or your life—because inevitably it will take all three, if you continue."

An Important Step

"You learn how to smoke. You can learn how to not smoke," says White. "Teens need to know they have the ability to control their habit and can get help. It's hard work and takes a commitment. But, you can start to stop and keep stopping—until you stop [for good]."

Says Dr. Antonia C. Novello, a former U.S. Surgeon General, "Quitting smoking represents the single most important step that smokers can take to enhance the length and the quality of their lives."

A Former Smoker Looks Back

Dale Pray

Dale Pray, a former smoker, says smokers surrounded him from childhood. He recalls childhood memories, such as when his mother used cigarette smoke to soothe his painful earaches. He also describes how peer pressure led him to start smoking regularly at the age of twelve. Pray offers this narrative on his personal website as a warning to others.

I was first exposed to cigarettes when I was in the womb. Mom was a smoker at the age of 16. She quit school and went to work in the shoe shop like many of her peers did at that time. You didn't need an education to work, jobs were everywhere. Cigarettes were cheap and a large percentage of the population smoked. It seemed that the worst health hazard from smoking at a young age back in that era was that perhaps it would "stunt your growth." Mom never grew more than 5 feet tall. (Probably just a coincidence.) Mom and Dad got married in February of 1954, shortly after I was "on the way." Folks back then were not aware of the dangers and risks associated with smoking while pregnant. So many of us smokers got our first dose of nicotine thru the umbilical cord.

Reprinted from Dale Pray, "How I Got Hooked on Cigarettes," an online article found at www.megalink.net/~dale/quitcig2.html. Reprinted with permission from the author.

Surrounded by Smoke

From my birth in December of 1954 my odyssey with cigarettes began with exposure to secondhand smoke. Everywhere you went there was someone smoking. No one gave it a thought that perhaps the smoke-filled rooms and automobiles might harm the ones that didn't smoke. Smoking just seemed to me as a normal thing for grownups to do. I fully expected to become a smoker myself someday. Thanks to some candy manufacturers, I was able to simulate smoking by buying some candy cigarettes. I was very careful to hold it between my fingers like a real one and put the filter end in my mouth. The end you would light, if it was a real one, was dyed red to simulate the lit end. Candy cigarettes even came in the popular brands and similar styles that the real ones came in. This helped in establishing a loyalty to a particular brand at a young age I suppose.

> Many of us smokers got our first dose of nicotine thru the umbilical cord.

Now that I reflect back, I seem to recall a toy cigarette that would emit simulated smoke when a kid blew through it. I guess it made me feel good to emulate something that adults did.

I recall getting my first feeling of comfort from cigarette smoke when I was a toddler of perhaps 4 or 5 years of age. I suffered from horrendously painful earaches. I would wake up in the middle of the night with my inner ear throbbing with pain. I remember the sound of drumming, snapping and crackling inside my ears as the drainage from the ear infection would flow and the tissues were swelling. Inevitably I would cry out to Mom. Mom would take me in her arms and bring me to her rocking chair in the living room. She would light up a cigarette, inhale, then very gently blow the warm smoke into my hurting little ear. This always seemed to help relieve the pain, or at least make it bearable. After the cigarette treatment Mom would put a few warm drops of baby oil in my ear, insert a wad of cotton and rock me until I fell asleep. An act of love and compassion from mother to child that meant a lot to me back then, but would probably not be considered a good thing to do in case of earache now.

The Start of a Habit

I got my first actual puff on a real cigarette at around age 10. I recall a real boring afternoon visiting some relatives with my folks. The relatives didn't have any children at home. They had all grown up and moved on. So there I was bored out of my gourd, when I decided I would take a nap in the car while my folks finished their visit. That's when I noticed an ashtray with some partially smoked butts and a cigarette lighter, right there in front of me. Curiosity got the better of me. I chose one of the longest stubs I could find, straightened out the kinks where it had been crushed out, and put it to my lips. I pushed in the cigarette lighter handle, like I had seen Mom do many times, and waited for the familiar click that signaled when the lighter was hot enough to light a cig. I took the cherry red tip of the lighter and placed it on the end of the cigarette butt and sucked. I got a mouthful of the foul hot smoke, blew it out, and wondered what the attraction of cigarettes was supposed to be. They tasted awful. I don't think I tried them again for several more years.

When I was around 12, I started delivering *TV Guides* to homes around town to earn some money. I would always be on the look out for bottles to cash in for the deposit. I also got an allowance from my folks for doing chores around the house. It was great having some coin in my pocket to buy Slim Jims, popsicles and Beatle trading cards. One summer afternoon I was out delivering my *TV Guides*. One of my customers had a boy a year older than I was, Jim was his name. His parents were not home, but Jim invited me in to hang out with him and his buddies. They were playing cribbage for cigarettes. I didn't know how to play

> Peer pressure, wanting to be cool and do grownup things gave me the incentive to keep on inhaling.

cribbage but Jim offered to teach me and even gave me a few cigarettes to get started. Well I must have had one massive case of beginners luck, because an hour or so later I was the owner of a pile of cigarettes. I was also the owner of a brand new habit that would haunt me for many years. I was well on my way to becoming addicted to cigarettes.

> 90% of smokers begin before they're 21, and 60% before they're 14!

I didn't inhale at first, just sucked in the smoke and blew it out. One day another of my smoking buddies asked me if I inhaled. I said no, I really didn't realize that was part of smoking. He said to take a puff on the cig and then just breathe it back into the lungs. I tried it and choked and coughed and got dizzy like every one does when they first inhale. But I was determined to keep it up until I could smoke with the best of them. Why didn't I take that strong hint that my body was trying to give me, that *cigarettes are bad for you.* Let's face it the choke, cough and gag reflex is a part of our bodies for a good reason. It is a body's natural defense mechanism shouting *nasty stuff, foul air, unnatural thing to do.* . . . Yet peer pressure, wanting to be cool and do grownup things gave me the incentive to keep on inhaling till I got it right and became thoroughly addicted to the proverbial cancer stick.

Further Recollections

Winstons were my cigarette of choice. I remember a childhood version of the Winston song. "Winston tastes good like a cigarette should. No flavor, no taste, just a 30 cent waste". I used to buy Winstons for my Mom at the neighborhood stores. So naturally I bought the same brand so as not to arise suspicion that I was the one I was buying cigarettes for. Even back in the mid-60s it was not considered good form for a 12 or 13 year old kid to be smoking. So we would find places around town that were out of site and a kid could smoke away from the disapproving eyes of adults. Under the bridge in the center of town or up on the railroad trestle were good spots to smoke. At any given time there was always someone there you could smoke and joke with. Sharing a cigarette was kind of a social thing. You could always "bum a cig" if you needed one or you would give one to someone else who needed one. I very seldom had to bum, as I had my own *TV Guide* route, and eventually went on to sell newspapers as well. Some of the guys used to steal their cigs, either from a store or from their parents. Of course I never did, being the darling little angel that I was. . . .

By the time I was 16 I had permission to smoke, as was common back then. I am sure my folks knew I had been smoking for quite some time, but now I could smoke in the house. I didn't have to hide it, except at school. I remember sharing a cigarette with buddies in the bathroom. Someone would stand guard at the door scanning for teachers. While the other ones would huff down a quick cigarette. You had to be quick and make every hit count, especially if your next class was way on the other end of school. I was smoking over a pack of cigs a day.

The tobacco industry loses close to 5,000 customers every day in the US alone— including 3,500 who manage to quit and about 1,200 who die. The most promising "replacement smokers" are young people: 90% of smokers begin before they're 21, and 60% before they're 14!

Not Ready to Quit

Kevin Simpson

Many teen smokers are ambivalent about their habit. They may not enjoy smoking, but don't wish to stop, either. One such teenager, Jeff Eastridge, is profiled below by *Denver Post* staff writer Kevin Simpson. Eastridge started smoking when he was thirteen as a way to fit in at a new school. Although his mother disapproves and he had to quit playing football because of his habit, Eastridge is not yet ready or able to stop smoking.

J eff Eastridge stands at ground zero in the tobacco wars: He is 15, and he smokes.

He has heard and read just enough to know that—on the surface, at least—it's all about him: the congressional skirmishing, the presidential posturing, the advertising dollars Big Tobacco plowed into public debate on [June 1998's] failed legislation to curb teen smoking.

He sees the big picture. But he lives the little one.

Quitting Is Not Top Priority

For Jeff, who just finished his freshman year at Littleton, Colorado's Arapahoe High School, kicking the habit is definitely on his to-do list, but in terms of immediacy, it ranks somewhere be-

Reprinted from Kevin Simpson, "Teen Sees Will to Quit Go Up in Smoke," *Denver Post*, June 25, 1998. Reprinted with permission from the *Denver Post*.

hind lining up lawn-mowing jobs so he can scrape up some summertime spending money.

"I feel like I want to quit bad enough that I will—eventually," Jeff says, figuring that he might be able to stop by the end of the summer, or maybe by the end of high school. "I'll just keep quitting until it's permanent."

> "I couldn't imagine myself being a smoker, but I couldn't imagine myself being a non-smoker. I had this mental addiction."

Enrolled in a quit-smoking program at Arapahoe this spring, Jeff tried cold-turkey and failed after four miserable days, which was when he realized for the first time that his grip on the habit couldn't quite match the grip his habit had on him.

"In the mornings, I'd get dizzy around first period, like I was floating," he says, detailing the withdrawal symptoms that caught him by surprise. "I'd be sitting there in class and, like, have to move my legs. My hands were cold. My feet were cold. I couldn't imagine myself being a smoker, but I couldn't imagine myself being a nonsmoker. I had this mental addiction."

Why Jeff Started Smoking

It started two years ago with all the usual trappings of adolescent anxiety and the desire to fit in. Just arrived to the suburbs from Denver, Jeff found no immediately comfortable place in the middle-school social strata. Almost by default, he hung with the smokers, even though he'd never taken a puff.

He didn't hold out for long.

They told him not to worry if he coughed at first. Everybody hacked the first few times. So he fired up a Marlboro and choked on his first drag. He thought it was gross, said so, didn't light another.

"After about a week, though, they got me to do it again," he says. "I'm usually not persuaded like that. I think it was just the time in my life—new neighborhood, new friends, cliquish school.

I wanted to be accepted real bad."

Within two weeks, he was smoking daily. By the end of eighth grade, he was a pack-a-day regular. A 13-year-old Marlboro Man.

The Parents' Perspective

His parents weren't pleased. Smoking remains forbidden in the home.

"You start out by demanding that he quit," says his mother, Eileen. "But it's really hard to know how to react to it, because he doesn't seem to be able to quit, and we can't just hate him for it."

Initially, they grounded Jeff. Then they made him research the effects of smoking and write an essay. All that did was make him angry.

His mother felt powerless. Eileen had been a smoker once, starting at about the same age Jeff did and continuing well into adulthood, when she finally mustered the willpower to quit.

But she remembers the struggle, which is why she tempers her concern for Jeff's health with a dose of empathy. Still, family history is family history—and both of Jeff's grandfathers died from smoking-related illnesses.

"I'm not sure he wants to quit," Eileen says. "If he wanted to, I'd be willing to spring for a patch or gum or something. But he doesn't seem to have the desire to quit. We don't talk about it a whole lot.

> "It's hard for teens to really see that tobacco is doing anything to them."

It's a subject we really don't know how to address. . . . I feel like I have a secret, and I'm trying to pass it on, but he won't listen."

Smoking or Football

Although Jeff was slow to realize it, his smoking soon slipped beyond his control. Last fall, at the start of his freshman year, he found himself choosing between cigarettes and something he truly loves—football.

After he was spotted smoking while wearing a team jersey, Jeff says, he learned from fellow freshmen that the whole varsity team was looking for him—a peer-pressure threat of unspecified consequences. Jeff didn't wait to find out. He quit the team.

"There's nothing I love more than football," he says now. "And I ended up quitting it because of a little piece of paper with a drug in the middle."

> Although [Jeff] says ads had little to do with his own reasons for starting to smoke, the ubiquitous reminders often pick and prod his craving.

[In spring 1998], he heard about a quit-smoking program on the school announcements. The first meeting offered free food, an undeniable enticement to a teenage boy.

He met Mary Bearman, a psychotherapist—and, for 27 years, a smoker—who set up the Centura Adolescent Tobacco Cessation Program at Arapahoe High.

"It's a pediatric disease," says Bearman, citing statistics that claim 90 percent of smokers start before they're 18. "Once they have them, they have them. It's hard for teens to really see that tobacco is doing anything to them. It's difficult to get them to quit for the same reason it's hard to get kids to buckle seat belts, or protect themselves when they're sexually active. It's not immediate to them."

The group met every day after school from early spring until the last week of classes, and even after Bearman left, teacher volunteers provided a support network. But nothing could have prepared Jeff for the sheer physical backlash from his own body, the symptoms that, for the first time, introduced him to the concept of addiction.

The Struggle to Quit

"I didn't think they'd be so extreme as they were," Jeff says. "I thought I'd be able to put them in the back of my mind. But it was a lot worse than that. I didn't think I'd smoked long enough to have withdrawal. I always thought I'd quit when I got tired of it, that I wouldn't let it get to that point.

"I still think it's under control. I'll just keep quitting until it works."

Jeff says cigarette advertisements haven't helped. Although he says ads had little to do with his own reasons for starting to smoke, the ubiquitous reminders often prick and prod his craving.

"This is the one that gets me," he says, flipping to a two-page magazine spread of the Marlboro Man in working pose, rough-hewn in his cowboy gear, his face obscured by the wide brim of his hat. There is no text, but Jeff reads the message.

"It's not saying anything, but the guy is smoking. Plus, that's my brand. It makes me feel like it's me, like I need to be doing that."

For about a week now, Jeff has tried to limit himself to just three cigarettes a day. His friends who smoke try to support him. They don't offer their own.

But sometimes he asks. And sometimes he tells his mother he's going for a walk, and she knows.

He didn't take a puff at all Sunday, and it wasn't until late Monday night that he relented and lit up two in succession. The second one made him feel guilty.

Now, the object of the tobacco wars has gone 12 hours since his last cigarette. "My palms are a little sweaty," Jeff says. "And my hands are cold."

Dealing with a Family of Smokers

Trenée Bryant Broughton

Sometimes teenagers' principal exposure to smoking comes not from their peers or the media, but from their families. Teenager Trenée Bryan Broughton does not smoke, but many members of her family do. Broughton has not been able to convince her family to quit despite the effects that secondhand smoke has had on her and her grandmother, such as dizziness and difficulty breathing. She vows that when she has children, they will be raised in a smoke-free environment. Broughton writes for *New Youth Connections*, a magazine written by and for teenagers.

One day a few years ago some friends and I were talking about a guy we thought was cute, but he smoked. "That's the only problem with him," one friend said, "His breath stinks from that cigarette smoke. If he didn't smoke, he would be perfect."

I knew then that if I ever started smoking it would make my friends look at me in a negative way.

Not long after this, I was in class when a friend asked if she could borrow a pencil. "Sure, look in my bookbag," I said.

Before my friend got the pencil, she asked me, "Have you

Reprinted from Trenée Bryant Broughton, "A Family of Buttheads," *New Youth Connections*, December 1995. Reprinted with permission from Youth Communication.

been smoking reefer?"

I was astonished. What made her ask such a question? "Of course not," I replied.

"Then why does it smell like smoke?" she asked.

Smokers in the House

Then it hit me. My family's cigarette smoke had seeped into my bookbag. People would now think that I was smoking because my bookbag smelled like Vantage Blues and Newports. I went home that afternoon feeling angry.

Out of the eight people I live with, four smoke—my dad, my aunt, and two uncles. I'm with them every day from the time I get home from school until the time I go to sleep. I smell their smoke after dinner and when we watch TV. Even

> I knew . . . that if I ever started smoking it would make my friends look at me in a negative way.

when we go out to eat or have picnics at the park, they always have to have a cigarette at some point. I hate the feeling of their thick toxic smoke creeping down to my lungs, expanding around them like foam.

I told my family what happened at school and complained to them about how their smoking affects my life, too. I begged them to stop smoking. I got the same answer that I got every other time I asked them to quit.

Refuses to Quit

They say, "I'm going to start cutting down on the cigarettes." But they never do.

Sometimes my aunt or my father will ask me to get them a cigarette, or they will leave the room and forget to put their cigarettes out, so I have to do it. Just touching their cigarettes makes me cringe.

Afterwards, I wash my hands frantically, trying to get the nauseating scent off.

My grandmother started wearing a surgical mask around the house to keep other people's smoke from going down her lungs. She used to be a smoker, too. Then, right around the time my friend smelled smoke in my bag, the doctor told my grandmother she had to quit—immediately. And she did, no ifs, ands or buts about it. She tells my aunt, my father and my two uncles all the time that their smoke is bothering her, but they still won't stop.

Secondhand Smoke and Its Health Effects

What is secondhand smoke?
- Secondhand smoke is a mixture of the smoke given off by the burning end of a cigarette, pipe, or cigar, and the smoke exhaled from the lungs of smokers.
- The mixture contains more than 4,000 substances, more than 40 of which are known to cause cancer in humans or animals and many of which are strong irritants.
- Secondhand smoke is also called environmental tobacco smoke (ETS); exposure to secondhand smoke is called involuntary smoking, or passive smoking.

Secondhand smoke can cause lung cancer in nonsmokers.
- Secondhand smoke has been classified by the U.S. Environmental Protection Agency (EPA) as a known cause of lung cancer in humans (Group A carcinogen).
- Passive smoking is estimated by EPA to cause approximately 3,000 lung cancer deaths in nonsmokers each year.

Environmental Protection Agency, "Secondhand Smoke," July 1993.

Once at a school fair I got photos of what the lung looks like when it is exposed to cigarette smoke, and showed them to my family. They took one look at them and continued to smoke.

My aunt thinks that smoking is good for her nerves. She says that it relaxes her. To my father, it's "just a habit" that he started when he was around 18, to look more grown-up.

A couple of months ago, when my father was putting out one of his cigarettes because I asked him to, he told me, "I better not ever catch you with a cigarette in your mouth."

He meant it like, "You're bothering me so much that if you ever pick up the habit, I'm going to badger you the same way you're badgering me." But the bad thing was, he wasn't taking the risks of smoking seriously. I looked at him and said, "You don't even have to worry about me ever smoking."

Dangerous to Nonsmokers

I'm convinced that smoking is deadly and can cause more harm than people think. Why else would the government make it illegal to smoke in public areas like restaurants, airplanes, and movie theaters? I'm glad there are anti-smoking laws because it's not only family members who bother me when they smoke. I hate it when I'm outside and I happen to be right behind some smoker who puffs cigarettes right in my face and in my nose. I get very dizzy and feel like kicking the person in front of me. I try to inhale to just get fresh air in, but it's impossible. Smokers are killing themselves slowly, taking us non-smokers with them.

> I'm convinced that smoking is deadly and can cause more harm than people think.

I promised myself a long time ago that when I have my own house, I will create a smoke-free environment for me and my children. I will eliminate the risk of becoming a middle-aged woman with bad breath, lung cancer and nicotine fits by never putting a cigarette in my mouth. I have the right to live a healthy life and I want to live for a very long time.

I'm leaving for college next year and I will probably live in a dorm. I'm looking forward to getting away from my family's smoke during the school year. But I still really want my relatives to see the importance of providing a smoke-free home for themselves, my grandmother, my younger sister and me.

Nowadays I draw attention to their habit by running to open a window when they light up or turning my head away abruptly. They usually puff a couple more times, but then sometimes they'll put the cigarettes out. At those particular moments, I feel that they understand what I've been complaining about for so long and I'm encouraged to continue seeking ways to get them to quit smoking.

Maybe someday they will listen.

Chapter 3

The Effects
of Smoking

Smoking Has Serious Health Effects

Paul H. Brodish

Teenagers often think that health problems caused by smoking will not occur until well into adulthood and that they can easily quit before that time. Paul H. Brodish warns otherwise, noting that teens have great difficulty quitting and do suffer irreversible health effects. Teen smokers' respiratory health is particularly at risk, because smoking at a young age impedes lungs from achieving full function and development. Furthermore, smoking-related health problems can occur long after a smoker quits. Brodish is a research specialist in North Carolina.

Cigarettes damage the body—gradually and insidiously—in a number of different ways. Over the years, the American Council on Science and Health and others have documented the effects. Our purpose here is to address the following key questions:

• Does a cigarette smoker who quits return to the health profile of a nonsmoker? If so, when?

• If the smoker's profile does not fully return to that of presmoking days, what effects are irreversible—and when do they

Reprinted from Paul Brodish, "The Irreversible Health Effects of Cigarette Smoking," an online article found at www.acsh.org/publications/booklets/iesmoke.html. Reprinted with permission from the American Council on Science and Health (ACSH), 1995 Broadway, 2nd Floor, New York, NY 10023-5860. Visit ACSH online at www.acsh.org.

become irreversible?

• What damage can be reversed—and to what extent?

There Are Long-Term Effects

One popular argument the scientific community often makes to encourage smokers to quit stems from the conjecture that all of the health effects of smoking are reversible shortly after cessation, regardless of the duration or intensity of the smoking exposure. Unfortunately, this conjecture is not true. Teenagers, in particular, may be overly complacent about smoking because they believe— incorrectly—that they can smoke for a few years and then quit without suffering any long-term effects. This complacency is especially troubling in light of the recent finding, reported by the Centers for Disease Control and Prevention (CDC), that teen smoking rates have increased by nearly a third within the last six years.

> The quitting success rate among teenagers is very low.

Teen smokers who believe that all the health hazards of cigarettes will disappear in a puff of smoke when they quit—who assume that smoking from, say, age 16 to age 28 will have no long-term effects—often fall back on an "I can always quit tomorrow" (or next month or next year) philosophy. They trust— mistakenly—that any adverse health consequences they may incur during their smoking years will disappear when, eventually, they stop lighting up. But another recent study has reported that the quitting success rate among teenagers is very low: Less than 16 percent of the 633 teen smokers in the study were able to kick the habit. This report will summarize the data on this vital—but rarely covered—topic.

What this report will not do is reexamine issues treated thoroughly elsewhere—issues such as the known deleterious health effects tobacco has in active smokers. These effects—cancers of various organs, heart attacks and strokes, ulcers, and infertility among them—are all major health issues; all provide good reasons not to smoke. They are, however, outside the scope of "irreversible effects" we intend to cover here.

Cigarettes and Public Health

Cigarette smoking is the leading cause of preventable death in the United States. It accounts for almost 500,000 deaths per year, or one in every five deaths. Cigarette smoking contributes to a remarkable number of diseases, including coronary heart disease, stroke, chronic obstructive pulmonary disease, peripheral vascular disease, peptic ulcer disease, and many types of cancer. Of the 46 million smokers in the United States, 34 percent try to quit each year—but less than 10 percent succeed.

According to the CDC, approximately 80 percent of current adult smokers began smoking before their 18th birthday. Each day over 3,000 teenagers light up for the first time. Most teens are aware of smoking's hazards, but few are worried about them. Moreover, most teen smokers quickly become addicted to nicotine: They report that they want to quit but are unable to do so. And teen smokers experience high relapse rates and debilitating withdrawal symptoms.

The bottom line is that smoking is costly, both to individual smokers and to society as a whole: Recent long-term studies indicate that about half of all regular cigarette smokers will eventually die from their addiction.

> Teen smokers experience high relapse rates and debilitating withdrawal symptoms.

With smoking, the reversibility of health effects is influenced by many factors. Among those factors are smoking exposure (the number of cigarettes per day and the duration of smoking) and physiologic susceptibility. The presence of other diseases, genetic variables, and even nutritional factors also enter into susceptibility assessment. Quitting brings benefits at any age, but there are "threshold" amounts of smoking that irreversibly increase the risk for some diseases.

The good news is that quitting prolongs life and reduces the risk of tobacco-related cancers, myocardial infarction, cerebrovascular disease, and chronic obstructive pulmonary disease (COPD). Current knowledge of the irreversible effects of smoking, organized by organ systems, follows.

Smoking Damages the Lungs

Smoking directly irritates and damages the respiratory tract. Each year a one-pack-a-day smoker smears the equivalent of a cup of tar over his or her respiratory tract. This irritation and damage cause a variety of symptoms, including bad breath, cough, sputum production, wheezing, and respiratory infections such as bronchitis and pneumonia. These effects can be reduced, but not entirely reversed, by quitting.

Smoking is the principal risk factor for developing COPD—i.e., chronic bronchitis and emphysema. Emphysema is characterized by permanent structural changes in the lung tissue. The deterioration in lung function associated with COPD is directly related to duration of smoking and the number of cigarettes smoked ("pack-years"). Smoking during childhood not only increases the risk of developing COPD in adulthood but also lowers the age of its onset.

Cigarette smoking during childhood and adolescence increases the number and severity of respiratory illnesses. It also causes retardation in the rate of lung development and in the level of maximum lung function—and retardation in lung growth during childhood means that the lungs may never attain normal function and development.

> Cigarette smoking during childhood and adolescence increases the number and severity of respiratory illnesses.

Everyone—smoker and nonsmoker alike—experiences a slow decline in lung function starting at about age 30. In smokers this gradual decline starts both from a lower baseline and at an earlier age. Smokers suffer from decreased lung reserve: They are unable to run—or even walk—as far or as fast as their peers who have never smoked. Smokers thus can expect permanently impaired lung function relative to their nonsmoking peers.

With sustained abstinence from smoking, the rate of decline in pulmonary function among smokers returns to normal; but lung reserve remains decreased relative to those who have never smoked. Quitting improves pulmonary function by about 5 percent within a few months of cessation, and COPD mortality rates decline among quitters versus continuing smokers. A study in more than 10,000 boys and girls aged 10 to 18 confirmed that cigarette smoking is associated with mild airway obstruction and slowed growth of lung function. The study, which covered a period of 15 years, also demonstrated that girls are more susceptible than boys to smoking's adverse effects on the growth of lung function.

Increased Rates of Lung Cancer

Smoking-induced chronic irritation of the respiratory lining and the wide variety of carcinogens in cigarette smoke induce permanent changes in the cells lining the respiratory tract. These changes can lead to cancer. Cigarette smoking is, in fact, the major cause of lung cancers of all major histologic types.

During the past half century, lung cancer rates have dramatically increased in women, to the extent that lung cancer is now the leading cause of cancer death in women, exceeding both breast cancer and colon cancer. (Smoking has, of course, been the leading cause of cancer death in men for decades.) This increased female mortality parallels the increase in cigarette smoking among women.

Smoking cessation reduces lung cancer risk by 30 percent to 50 percent 10 years after quitting, and the risk continues to decline with further abstinence. The risk in ex-smokers always remains increased compared to that in nonsmokers, however. It is now known that almost 50 percent of all lung cancers are diagnosed in ex-smokers, and this finding is not surprising in view of the fact that there exist a "plethora of studies demonstrating a lag between smoking initiation and increased incidence of lung cancer of several decades."

One study noted that 75 percent of ex-smokers showed changes in their DNA indicative of precancerous lesions, as compared to only 3 percent of people who had never smoked. At the May 1998 meeting of the American Lung Association, data were presented showing that former smokers continued to develop lung cancer at rates 11 to 33 times higher than nonsmokers. The data also showed that the shorter the time since quitting, the higher was the ex-smoker's risk. Increased risk was still noted in former smokers after more than 20 years of abstinence, however.

> Girls are more susceptible than boys to smoking's adverse effects on the growth of lung function.

Heart and Circulation

Premature coronary heart disease (CHD) is one of the most important medical consequences of smoking. Smoking acts both independently of and synergistically with other major risk factors for heart disease. Sadly, sudden death may be the first sign of CHD—and sudden death is four times more likely to occur in young male cigarette smokers than in nonsmokers. Women who use both cigarettes and oral contraceptives increase their risk of developing CHD tenfold. The excess risk of coronary heart disease is halved in quitters (as compared to continuing smokers) one year after cessation, but the risk level doesn't return to that of nonsmokers until 15 years after quitting.

In a study of atherosclerosis, the progression of fatty deposits in the carotid artery was found to be dependent on total pack-years of tobacco exposure, rather than on the patient's current smoking status. This finding indicates that atherosclerosis progression may also be cumulative and irreversible, at least after some degree of baseline exposure.

Cerebrovascular accident (CVA), or stroke, causes brain damage that usually leaves its victims with permanent disabilities. Smokers' excess risk for stroke appears to return to that of nonsmokers within 5 to 15 years of cessation. One recent study suggests, however, that an ex-smoker's risk remains high for at least 20 years after cessation. In addition, it was recently learned that the incidence of "silent strokes"—events that are harbingers of both severe strokes and dementia—is increased in anyone who has ever smoked.

Smoking Related Deaths, 1990–94

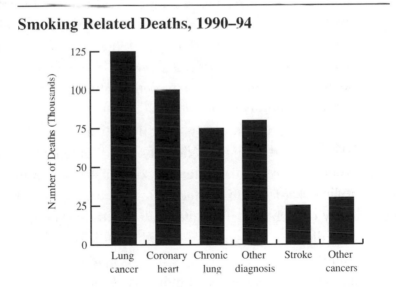

National Institute on Drug Abuse, "Nicotine Addiction."

Finally, smoking is a strong risk factor for several types of blood-vessel disease. Smoking causes poor circulation to the legs by narrowing the blood vessels that supply these extremities. Quitting reduces, but does not eliminate, this risk. Once it becomes symptomatic, such circulatory impairment often requires surgical intervention. . . .

Smoking's Effects on Pregnancy

Infertility is more common among smokers but is not irreversible. The damage done to smokers' babies during pregnancy often is irreversible, however. Smoking during pregnancy is associated with dire consequences for the baby as a fetus, as a newborn, and even as a child. Recognition of the evidence of this damage has prompted researchers to designate it as "fetal tobacco syndrome."

Miscarriage is two to three times more common in smokers, as are stillbirths due to fetal oxygen deprivation and placental abnormalities induced by the carbon monoxide and nicotine in cigarette smoke. Smokers have a fourfold risk of having a low birth-weight baby; such babies are more likely than normal-weight babies to have impaired physical, emotional, and intellectual development. The authors of a 1996 study found that women who smoked during pregnancy were 50 percent more likely to have a child with mental retardation of unknown cause than were nonsmoking women.

Sudden infant death syndrome is significantly associated with smoking, as is impaired lung function at birth. Women who quit smoking as late as the first trimester may diminish some of these risks, but the risk of certain congenital malformations—such as cleft palate—is increased even in women who quit early in pregnancy.

> Smoking during pregnancy is associated with dire consequences for the baby.

Smoking causes premature facial wrinkling through vasoconstriction of the capillaries of the face (vasoconstriction decreases the flow of oxygen and nutrients to facial skin cells). The effect of this reduced blood flow is visible in deep crow's feet radiating from the corners of the eyes and pale, grayish, wrinkled skin on the cheeks. These effects may emerge after as few as five years of smoking and are largely irreversible, except through costly and traumatic facial surgery.

Quitting Does Not End the Dangers

There should be no illusions as to the dangers of cigarettes. The combination of a highly addictive, pharmacologically active substance—nicotine—and an array of noxious chemicals cunningly packaged in a highly efficient delivery mechanism can permanently and drastically affect health.

People who smoke for as brief a period as 10 years show a substantially higher rate of death, disease, and disability. Risks to the respiratory system, especially, and risks of cancer continue to plague the ex-smoker for years after quitting. Smokers should not delude themselves that they can smoke safely for 10 to 15 years and then—if they are among the lucky few who *can* quit—become as healthy and risk-free as if they had never smoked at all.

> People who smoke for as brief a period as 10 years show a substantially higher rate of death, disease, and disability.

This report has been brief—much briefer, in fact, than we would have liked. The main reason for that brevity, simply stated, is that there should be much more good, scientific information out there than there is about the real risks ex-smokers face. Almost all of the studies conducted on the health hazards of smoking simply compare smokers with nonsmokers; the studies do not differentiate between never-smokers and ex-smokers. (The risks faced by smokers are well-documented; for a truly comprehensive guide to those risks, see the groundbreaking ACSH [American Council on Science and Health] book, *Cigarettes: What the Warning Label Doesn't Tell You.*)

More controlled studies—studies assessing long-term results in people who have quit smoking at various times in the past— are needed. Until such studies are performed and reported, researchers can access valuable data on the irreversible health effects of smoking through already-available databases such as those of the Framingham study and the Mayo Clinic.

In summary, the following irreversible health effects have been proven to be associated with smoking:

- Retardation in the rate of lung development and lung function—i.e., decreased lung reserve—in childhood and adolescent smokers, as well as a markedly increased risk of developing COPD.
- Cancer risk: 75 percent of ex-smokers show DNA changes suggestive of tumor development; 50 percent or more of lung cancers are now being diagnosed in ex-smokers.
- Circulatory impairment to the heart, brain, and legs.
- Visual impairment and loss.
- Vocal-cord polyps (growths) and hoarseness.
- Bone mineral loss (osteoporosis), hip fractures, and spinal arthritis.
- Serious health consequences for children born to smoking mothers.
- Premature facial wrinkling and graying of the skin after as few as five years of smoking.

This report is intended for everyone—smokers, never-smokers, and ex-smokers alike—but it is aimed particularly at those who have not yet become addicted to tobacco. To everyone we say, Remember: Only 20 percent of smokers who try to quit are successful on a long-term basis; for four out of five of those who take up smoking, the very decision to begin is itself irreversible.

The Dangers of Smokeless Tobacco

KidsHealth.org

Although its use does not harm the lungs, smokeless tobacco can be very hazardous to a teenager's health. Using smokeless tobacco—also known as chewing tobacco or spit tobacco—can lead to throat cancer and mouth cancer. Teenagers who use smokeless tobacco are misguided about its health effects and should take steps to quit. Kids-Health.org is an Internet site that provides health information about children.

"**M**an, I need something to zap these zits!"

"Her hair is so gorgeous; why can't mine look like that?"

"Forget it—I won't wear anything but Nikes."

"These jeans are way too tight."

"I wouldn't be caught dead shopping there."

"Dad, why can't we get a cooler car?"

If you're like a lot of other teenagers, you probably worry about how you look and where you're seen. So how do you think you look if you chew or "dip" tobacco? If you do, you build up so much saliva that you have to spit again and again. Not very sexy, wouldn't you agree?

But some teens think that indulging in spit tobacco (also known as smokeless tobacco) is cool. Some even think it's a safe alternative to *smoking.* They are wrong on both counts! Read on to find out more about the effects of spit tobacco.

What Is Spit Tobacco?

Spit tobacco, which baseball players started using to keep their mouths from getting dry in dusty ballparks, comes in two forms: *snuff,* a fine-grain tobacco that users "pinch" or "dip" between their lower lip and gum, and *chewing tobacco,* which is shredded tobacco leaves that users put between their cheek and gum. Sucking or chewing just a little of either allows nicotine to be absorbed into the bloodstream through the tissues in your mouth. You don't even need to swallow.

> Only 40% of kids think smokeless tobacco is harmful, compared to 77% who think cigarette smoking is.

But take a look. In addition to the addictive drug nicotine, you'll find these ingredients, and more, in spit tobacco:

- N-Nitrosamines (cancer-causing agents)
- Formaldehyde (a favorite preservative of dead things in biology class)
- Cadmium (used in car batteries)
- Arsenic (what you'd like to feed your worst enemies)
- Lead (the poisonous kind)
- Cyanide (another poison)
- Benzene (toxic liquid sometimes used as motor fuel)
- Polonium 210 (a radioactive element)

It's hard to imagine how this chemical soup could possibly enhance your image!

The ads for spit tobacco in sports magazines and the Smokeless Tobacco Council's denials of the connection between smokeless tobacco and cancer are working. One study, published in the Surgeon General's Report, says that only 40% of kids think smokeless tobacco is harmful, compared to 77% who think cigarette smoking is.

As many as 20% of high school boys and 2% of high school girls use smokeless tobacco says the Centers for Disease Control and Prevention. Of the 12 to 14 million American users, one third are under age 21, and more than half of those developed the habit before they were 13. Peer pressure, a desire to be mature or macho, and an attempt to imitate sports idols are just some of the reasons for starting the habit. Serious users often graduate from brands that deliver less nicotine to stronger ones. With each use, you need a little more of the drug to get the same feeling.

The Damage Caused by Smokeless Tobacco

During Bill Tuttle's second season with the Detroit Tigers, he took some chewing tobacco offered by a teammate. After chewing for just a week, he was hooked. By 1993, 37 years later, this tough, athletic pro-baseball player, idolized by young people, had lost much of his face to the cancer caused by his habit. Cancer cost him his jawbone, his right cheekbone, and his taste buds. It took four operations to remove cancerous tissue from his right cheek and complicated skin grafts to fill the gaping hole left by the surgery. He also lost his teeth and so much of his gum line that he couldn't even wear dentures (false teeth).

The cancers . . . from using spit tobacco are throat cancer and oral cancer, which can lead to loss of parts of your face, tongue, cheek, or lip.

You might be thinking that 37 years is more than twice your age, so why worry? But if you start or continue using spit tobacco now, your addiction could put you in Tuttle's unhappy league sooner than you think.

About 40 % of professional baseball players chew or dip, but each year the pressures mount for them to quit. Such baseball legends as Joe Garagiola, Hank Aaron, and Tuttle are stepping up the efforts in the National Spit Tobacco Education Program (NSTEP) to convince players, fans, and young people that smokeless tobacco is dangerous, addictive, and unsafe. "Smokeless does not mean harmless," Garagiola says. The Surgeon General has said there is "no safe use" of smokeless tobacco.

After finding a pre-cancerous lesion (or sore) on the inside of his lower lip, Philadelphia Phillies pitcher Curt Schilling, who had dipped for 15 years and tried to quit for 3, became more determined. "I have to quit," he said, "because I want to watch my kids grow up." After succeeding, he said that giving up snuff "was the hardest thing I've ever had to do."

> Spit tobacco actually delivers more nicotine than cigarettes.

The cancers Schilling feared from using spit tobacco are throat cancer and oral cancer, which can lead to loss of parts of your face, tongue, cheek, or lip.

Medical consequences of using spit tobacco include:
- cracking and bleeding lips and gums
- throat cancer and mouth cancer
- receding gums, which eventually can make your *teeth* fall out
- increased heart rate, high blood pressure, and irregular heart beats, all leading to a greater risk of heart attacks and brain attacks (stroke)

Not impressed? Think about the more immediate effects: *bad breath* and yellowish-brown stains on your teeth, not to mention the money required to maintain your habit.

How to Quit

The American Cancer Society says that spit tobacco actually delivers more nicotine than cigarettes. That might explain the intense struggle some users have when trying to quit. *Dr. Neil Izenberg,* adolescent medicine specialist and editor-in-chief of KidsHealth.org, emphasizes that you have to *want* to quit. If your motivation doesn't come from within, you're bound to fail.

There are many reasons to quit, and listing them might give you the motivation you need. For example, you don't want to turn off prospective dates with sores in your mouth. About 70% of spit tobacco users have them. Or how about getting your taste buds back? You also don't want to risk getting cancer; half of the people who get mouth cancer die from it. And you certainly don't want to become an addict who depends completely on the tobacco industry.

When you do quit, don't do it alone, advises Izenberg. Tell family and friends and enlist their support. When you have a craving, go for a walk with a friend or call a buddy to talk. Other strategies to consider include:

- nicotine gum or a patch (ask your doctor about these options first)
- substitutes, including tobacco-free, mint-leaf snuff; sugarless gum; hard candy; beef jerky; sunflower seeds; raisins; and dried fruit
- deep breathing
- a teeth cleaning
- activities for the healthier you: lifting weights, shooting baskets, or going for a swim
- a hot shower to relax
- a new pair of jeans or new hairstyle—something to spiff up your new, tobacco-free image

Realize that backsliding is common, but that your chances of success increase with each try. Plan ahead for tough moments by having gum or other substitutes handy. When you finally manage to quit, be sure and celebrate the new non-chewing you!

Smoking Does Not Cause Weight Loss

Sandra G. Boodman

Girls may smoke to stay thin, a belief tobacco companies exploit in their advertising. Sandra G. Boodman, a staff writer for the *Washington Post*, describes a study which proves that smoking does not aid in weight loss. While smokers do often gain weight after they quit, the effect is most noticeable among older smokers, not teenage girls. Weight control is at best a rare side effect of smoking.

For decades younger smokers, especially women who take up the habit as teenagers, have believed that cigarettes will help them lose or control their weight. Tobacco companies have exploited that association, marketing cigarettes named "slims" or "thins" and featuring models with commensurate body types.

It's not true—at least for those under 30.

A Disproved Notion

A federally funded study of nearly 4,000 young adults led by researchers from the University of Memphis has found that for people under age 30, smoking does not prevent weight gain. At best, according to a team of researchers led by psychologist Robert C. Klesges, the impact of smoking on body weight among young adults is minimal.

So why do so many people think smoking makes them thinner?

"That's because if you look at people who've smoked for many years, they weigh a bit less on average than nonsmokers," said Kenneth D. Ward, a member of the research team and a psychologist at the University of Memphis. The reasons for this weight disparity are unclear, Ward said, but it may result in part from the physiological effects of nicotine, which can speed metabolism.

"There's no question that smoking cigarettes definitely did not help younger people to lose weight," Ward said. "And smokers who do manage to quit gain more weight after they stop smoking than people who've never smoked."

Part of the difficulty in untangling the effect of smoking on weight may lie in one of the more unpleasant realities of aging: People typically gain weight as they get older. This weight gain may stem from inactivity, a slowing of metabolic rate, the consumption of more calories or a combination of these and other factors, Ward said.

> For people under age 30, smoking does not prevent weight gain.

The weight disparity between older smokers and nonsmokers may have helped fuel the notion that smoking is an effective method of weight control.

Ward and his colleagues noted in their study, published [in November 1998] in the *Journal of Consulting and Clinical Psychology,* that young people and women, especially teenage girls, mistakenly believe that smoking will help them remain, or become, thin.

Age Is a Factor

Smoking cigarettes does seem to mitigate this age-related weight gain, studies have found. Smokers in their fifties are on average thinner than their nonsmoking counterparts. Studies have found that a lifetime of smoking is associated with a weight difference of between 5 and 7 pounds. But the Memphis researchers said no such difference could be found in younger smokers.

"By the time people reach middle age," the authors wrote, "there are significant weight differences, not because smoking has created a weight loss but because it has attenuated weight gains. However, among white young adults (especially women), the groups most likely to smoke because of a perceived weight control benefit, these results suggested no weight gain attenuation."

"It's interesting that smoking doesn't have a big impact on weight control," said Simone A. French, a smoking researcher and associate professor of epidemiology at the University of Minnesota School of Public Health. "Among teenage girls who smoke, one of the beliefs is that smoking controls their weight. But it doesn't mean it caused them to start. I think that's a more complicated decision."

To test the relationship between smoking and body weight in young adults, researchers used data from the national study known as CARDIA, short for Coronary Artery Risk Development in Young Adults. The study, which was launched in 1985, included more than 5,110 whites and blacks between the ages of 18 and 30 living in Birmingham, Alabama; Minneapolis; Chicago; and Oakland, California.

> Young people and women, especially teenage girls, mistakenly believe that smoking will help them remain, or become, thin.

Participants were followed for seven years and smoking status was reassessed at intervals of 2, 5 and 7 years.

Racial Differences

The researchers found that at the beginning of the study, the weight of males did not differ significantly according to race.

There was, however, a measurable disparity among women:

African American women weighed significantly more than whites at the start of the study. The body mass index of black women was 25.9, while that of white women was 23.1.

Among blacks, those who quit smoking gained the most weight: an average of 28 pounds. African Americans who never smoked gained 18 pounds during the seven years of the study.

Among whites, those who quit also gained the most weight—nearly 21 pounds. But after seven years, whites who smoked continuously gained the same amount of weight as those who never smoked—about 11 pounds.

Yet for reasons that remain unclear to the authors, blacks who smoked continuously or who started smoking during the study were more likely to lose weight. Among whites, however, there was no such difference.

Weight loss during the seven years of the study was "relatively uncommon," the authors noted. Only about 4 percent of the group lost at least 11 pounds.

Ward said that his study suggests that smoking to control weight may actually backfire because if a smoker quits, he or she is likely to gain more weight than someone who never started in the first place.

This study, the authors suggest, may contain a message anti-smoking advocates can use in public service campaigns: Smoking doesn't make you thinner.

"Thus smoking prevention and public health messages should communicate that weight control is not a benefit of smoking, and if it does occur," the researchers wrote, "it is minimal and may take years to accrue."

Point of Contention: Is Smoking a Bad Habit or an Addiction?

The potentially addictive properties of nicotine—one of the key chemicals in tobacco—have been studied for decades. In 1988, former surgeon general C. Everett Koop proved that nicotine was an addictive drug. Koop's report was followed by other research that supported his findings, including a report issued in February 2000 by England's Royal College of Physicians, which declared nicotine to be as addictive as cocaine and heroin, and smoking to be a significant drug dependence. However, tobacco companies strongly disputed this conclusion for many years. As recently as 1994, tobacco company executives testified before Congress that nicotine was not addictive. Four years later, those companies reversed their testimony. Although tobacco companies now acknowledge that nicotine is addictive, many people argue that smokers can readily control their habit and should not be likened to drug addicts. Action on Smoking and Health, a national action and educational organization that fights for the rights of nonsmokers, argues that smoking is addictive. Judith Hatton, a researcher who works with the Freedom Organisation for the Right to Enjoy Smoking Tobacco, a British smoker's rights group, counters by asserting that smoking is a manageable habit.

Nicotine Is Addictive

Action on Smoking and Health

As long ago as 1942 there was significant medical evidence that nicotine is an addictive drug. That body of evidence has subsequently grown, and today it is a reasonable medical certainty that nicotine is addictive; so much so that it has been compared to heroin, alcohol and barbiturate addiction. Today, many cigarette smokers are in fact addicts. For this reason ASH has prepared the following summary of some of the more notable research in the area.

Why Nicotine Is Addictive

Tobacco use is addicting and nicotine is the active pharmacologic agent of tobacco that causes addictive behavior. It also causes physical dependence characterized by a withdrawal syndrome that usually accompanies nicotine abstinence. Evidence about the addictive nature of nicotine has been accumulating since 1942 when a medical researcher first identified the problem. Since that time many medical writers and journals have unequivocally classed smoking, and particularly cigarette-smoking, as an addiction for many people. Some physicians compare the addictive qualities of nicotine to heroin and barbiturates but others maintain that for many people cigarettes can be even more addictive than heroin, barbiturates or alcohol. Comparison can also be made between the use of hard drugs and smoking in various treatment programs and in the relapse rates for such programs. Aveena sativa, a withdrawal aid, has been noted to be somewhat effective in the aversive conditioning of both cigarette and heroin addiction. Apomorphine has been used in the treatment of

chronic alcoholism, drug addiction and addiction to cigarettes. As would be expected in addiction, the long-term
abstinence rates are not good. One of the factors making
nicotine so extremely addictive may be the tolerance
which smokers develop. Before he can enjoy inhaling
deeply, the novice must acquire a
degree of tolerance to the local irritation and autonomic side-effects
of nicotine. This is because nicotine is a poison. One-fortieth of a
gram of nicotine usually gives rise
to toxic symptoms in a nonsmoker. The toxic symptoms
consist of excessive "swimminess" (unlike vertigo), rapid
and forcible cardiac action, nausea, vomiting and fainting.
Once this tolerance has been established, most people
smoke to obtain nicotine and are unsatisfied by nicotine-
free cigarettes. Smokers unconsciously modify their puff
rate to maintain a steady nicotine intake when given high
or low nicotine cigarettes. Intravenous nicotine reduces
cigarette consumption significantly when compared with a
saline control. Nicotine shares with other dependence-
producing drugs the quality of acting as a primary rein-
forcer of behavior.

> It is a reasonable medical certainty that nicotine is addictive.

The 1988 Surgeon General's report, *The Health Consequences of Smoking: Nicotine Addiction* found that nicotine is a powerful pharmacologic agent that acts in the
brain and throughout the body. Nicotine readily crosses the
blood-brain barrier and accumulates in the brain shortly after it enters the body. Once in the brain it interacts with
specific receptors and alters brain energy metabolism in a
pattern consistent with the distribution of specific binding
sites for the drug. As a result, effects of nicotine on the

central nervous system occur rapidly after a puff of cigarette smoke or after absorption of nicotine from other routes of administration.

There is effective treatment available for the dependent smoker which requires behavioral intervention in addition to any pharmacologic agents that might be administered. Some of the behavioral intervention practices available are rapid smoking, relaxation training, social support and coping skills training. Making the facts about nicotine addiction known may not do much to help the already addicted smokers, but it will encourage more research into the problem of addiction and means to combat it.

Reprinted from Action on Smoking and Health, "Addiction to Nicotine," an online article found at http://ash.org/papers/h1.htm. Reprinted with permission.

Nicotine Is Not Addictive

Judith Hatton

"The smoker's behavior is not changed in any easily observable ways by smoking."

This admission, in *Addiction* (1994, pg 89), by M.A. Jarvis, of the Imperial Cancer Research Fund Health Behaviour Unit, shows what should, in a reasonable world, destroy the ever more popular theory that nicotine is a drug like heroin or cocaine. No-one could possibly say that smoking changes personality. A mild stimulating effect, increased mental alertness, combined, paradoxically enough, with a mild calming effect and relief of stress, are the most that have been established. Alcohol certainly can change the personality, and so can and mostly do all the other substances generally classed as drugs. So too can a great many

105

of the medical drugs prescribed for our ailments.

The periodical *What Doctors Don't Tell You* has published a list of the side effects of thirteen groups of commonly prescribed drugs. All but two of these have mental "side effects" ranging from depression (the commonest of all) to confusion, disorientaton, memory problems, delirium, hallucinations, and psychotic behaviour.

No Addictive Criteria

Dr Tage Voss, in *Smoking and Common Sense*, has given a list of the criteria for distinguishing between habituation and addiction. These run as follows:

1. Want
2. Freedom of choice
3. Psychological dependence
4. Physical dependence, increased tolerance, escalation of dosage, withdrawal, craving
5. Moral deterioration
6. Intellectual Reduction
7. Mental dissolution
8. Social collapse.

He points out that while alcohol and drugs fit all but one of these (freedom of choice), smoking does not, nor does it remove freedom of choice. Much as the anti-smokers would like to say that smoking causes mental dissolution or social collapse, they cannot. According to Dr. Sandy Macara, former chairman of the British Medical Association, "smokers could give up tomorrow, not today, if they wanted to."

The Ever-Broadening Definition of "Addiction"

"Addict. devote, apply habitually (to a practice), as his taste a. him, he addicts himself or his mind, he is addicted, to.

. . . So addict n., person addicted to specified drug & c (opium a.), addiction n." *The Concise Oxford Dictionary,* 1938.

"addict vt (usu.in passive) to give up (to) devote, apply habitually (to) -n. a slave to a habit or vice, esp. drugs . . . addiction the state of being addicted; a habit that has become impossible to break.- adj addictive tending to cause addiction, habit-forming." *Chambers Dictionary,* 1992.

Apply habitually to a practice: that is, smoking. Well, yes, smokers do. People apply themselves habitually to drinking tea, or coffee, to eating buns or chocolate, to gossiping, watching television, swimming, jogging, interfering in other people's lives, and many, many other things.

> Much as the anti-smokers would like to say that smoking causes mental dissolution or social collapse, they cannot.

And if they have to give them up they suffer according to the degree to which they have enjoyed them. And the difficulty in giving up is directly related to the degree of enjoyment. No-one could deny that. But "a habit that has become impossible to break": is there such a thing? Some habits are very difficult to break, and may even require help in doing so. Some people find it very difficult to give up any habit of any kind and may similarly need help. But eleven million smokers have given up in Britain, and 50 million in the US, in the last twenty years, the overwhelming majority without any "help" at all. That consumers can quit if they really want to was acknowledged recently by Sir Richard Doll, the man credited with discovering the link between smoking and lung cancer, when he declared: "What has been shown and it's now, I think, quite clear, is that practically everybody can give up if they want to . . . and most people do quite easily."

It is interesting, too, to note the strengthening of the dictionary definitions between 1938 and 1992: from "apply habitually to a practice," to "habit impossible to break." This seems to me to reflect the current attitude towards the individual: the denial of will-power. We are, in fact, dangerously close to accepting as gospel the old Marxist cliche: "circumstances make character." Since all democracies are ultimately based on the conception of the character of the individual as the foundation of society, this strikes at our roots.

Outlawing Habits

And so the argument runs: If there are individuals who cannot exercise will power in the face of advertising, then it must be banned. If some people cannot see violence or anti-social behaviour as depicted on film or television for what it is, then censorship must be introduced. And if there are people who find habits or "addictions" of any kind hard to break, then these habits must be outlawed.

In fact, we are ceasing to see society as composed of individuals most of whom are quite capable of getting on with their own lives with the minimum of interference. Instead we are becoming, in the eyes of our mostly self-appointed "masters" (and mistresses), the indistinguishable masses, all with the same characteristics (if any) and responding in exactly the same way to all pressures.

Professor Hans Eysenck, as one of the world's greatest psychologists, should be allowed the last word:

"[Smoking] is not an addiction because the term 'addiction' really has no scientific meaning; it is used in so many different ways that it is almost impossible to attach any meaning to it. This idea is not really controversial; there have been several books on it recently with people making exactly the same point. You could call sex addictive, or reading in my case, or playing tennis; you can call anything addictive which a person does routinely and which he would be sorry to stop doing and which might have all sorts of repercussions on his mental and physical life.

> ". . . there are very good reasons why people continue to smoke because it has consequences which to them are favourable, agreeable, positive—you don't have to posit a mysterious factor which makes them go on . . ."

Excerpted from Judith Hatton, "Smoking and Addiction," *Free Choice*, January/February 1996. Reprinted with permission from *Free Choice*.

Chapter 4

Responses to
Teen Smoking

Teen
Decisions

How to Quit

National Cancer Institute

The National Cancer Institute, an agency under the auspices of the National Institutes of Health, offers steps on how to quit smoking. Quitting can be very difficult, but smokers are most likely to end their habit if they know what to expect and have prepared for possible relapses. Smokers can quit successfully if they develop a clean, non-smoking environment around themselves and avoid situations where they might be tempted to smoke.

Many smokers have successfully given up cigarettes by replacing them with new habits without quitting "cold turkey," planning a special program, or seeking professional help.

The following approaches include many of those most popular with ex-smokers. Remember that successful methods are as different as the people who use them. What may seem silly to others may be just what you need to quit. So don't be embarrassed to try something new. These methods can make your own personal efforts a little easier.

Pick the ideas that make sense to you. And then follow through. You'll have a much better chance of success.

Preparing Yourself for Quitting

• Decide positively that you want to quit. Try to avoid negative thoughts about how difficult it might be.

Excerpted from National Cancer Institute, "Clearing the Air: How to Quit Smoking . . . and Quit for Keeps," September 1993.

• List all the reasons you want to quit. Every night before going to bed, repeat one of those reasons 10 times.

• Develop strong personal reasons in addition to your health and obligations to others. For example, think of all the time you waste taking cigarette breaks, rushing out to buy a pack, hunting for a light, etc.

• Begin to condition yourself physically: Start a modest exercise program; drink more fluids; get plenty of rest; and avoid fatigue.

> Quitting isn't easy, but it's not impossible either. More than 3 million Americans quit every year.

• Set a target date for quitting—perhaps a special day such as your birthday, your anniversary, or the Great American Smoke-out. If you smoke heavily at work, quit during your vacation so that you're already committed to quitting when you return. Make the date sacred and don't let anything change it. This will make it easy for you to keep track of the day you become a non-smoker and to celebrate that date every year.

Coping with Relapses

• Have realistic expectations—quitting isn't easy, but it's not impossible either. More than 3 million Americans quit every year.

• Understand that withdrawal symptoms are temporary. They usually last only 1–2 weeks.

• Knowing that most relapses occur in the first week after quitting, when withdrawal symptoms are strongest, and your body is still dependent on nicotine. Be aware that this will be your hardest time and use all your personal resources—willpower, family, friends, and the tips in this booklet—to get you through this critical period successfully.

• Know that most other relapses occur in the first 3 months after quitting, when situational triggers, such as a particularly stressful event, occur unexpectedly. These are the times when people reach for cigarettes automatically, because they associate smoking with relaxing. This is the kind of situation that's hard to prepare yourself for until it happens, so it's especially important to recognize it if it does happen. Remember that smoking is a habit, but a habit you can break.

• Realize that most successful ex-smokers quit for good only after several attempts. You may be one of those who can quit on your first try. But if you're not, don't give up. Try again.

Family and Friends

• Bet a friend you can quit on your target date. Put your cigarette money aside for every day you don't smoke and forfeit it if you smoke. (But if you do smoke, don't give up. Simply strengthen your resolve and try again.)

• Ask your friend or spouse to quit with you.

• Tell your family and friends that you're quitting and when. They can be an important source of support both before and after you quit.

Ways of Quitting

Switch Brands

• Switch to a brand you find distasteful.

• Change to a brand that is low in tar and nicotine a couple of weeks before your target date. This will help change your smoking behavior. However, do not smoke more cigarettes, inhale them more often or more deeply, or place your fingertips over the holes in the filters. These actions will increase your nicotine intake, and the idea is to get your body used to functioning without nicotine.

> Cutting down can help you quit, but it's not a substitute for quitting.

Cut Down the Number of Cigarettes You Smoke

• Smoke only half of each cigarette.

• Each day, postpone the lighting of your first cigarette 1 hour.

• Decide you'll only smoke during odd or even hours of the day.

• Decide beforehand how many cigarettes you'll smoke during the day. For each additional cigarette, give a dollar to your favorite charity.

• Change your eating habits to help you cut down. For example, drink milk, which many people consider incompatible with smoking. End meals or snacks with something that won't lead to a cigarette.

• Reach for a glass of juice instead of a cigarette for a "pick-me-up."

• Remember: Cutting down can help you quit, but it's not a substitute for quitting. If you're down to about seven cigarettes a day, it's time to set your target date to quit and get ready to stick to it.

Don't Smoke "Automatically"

• Smoke only those cigarettes you really want. Catch yourself before you light up a cigarette out of pure habit.

• Don't empty your ashtrays. This will remind you of how many cigarettes you've smoked each day, and the sight and the smell of stale cigarette butts will be very unpleasant.

> Don't think of never smoking again. Think of quitting in terms of 1 day at a time.

• Make yourself aware of each cigarette by using the opposite hand or putting cigarettes in an unfamiliar location or a different pocket to break the automatic reach.

• If you light up many times during the day without even thinking about it, try to look into a mirror each time you put a match to your cigarette—you may decide you don't need it.

Make Smoking Inconvenient and Unpleasant

• Stop buying cigarettes by the carton. Wait until one pack is empty before you buy another.

• Stop carrying cigarettes with you at home or at work. Make them difficult to get.

• Smoke only under circumstances that aren't especially pleasurable for you. If you like to smoke with others, smoke alone. Turn your chair to an empty corner and focus only on the cigarette you are smoking and all its many negative effects.

• Collect all your cigarette butts in one large glass container as a visual reminder of the filth made by smoking.

What to Do When You Quit

• Practice going without cigarettes.

• Don't think of never smoking again. Think of quitting in terms of 1 day at a time.

• Tell yourself you won't smoke today and then, don't.

• Clean your clothes to rid them of the cigarette smell, which can linger for a long time.

• Throw away all your cigarettes and matches. Hide your lighters and ashtrays.

• Visit the dentist and have your teeth cleaned to get rid of tobacco stains. Notice how nice they look and resolve to keep them that way.

• Make a list of things you'd like to buy for yourself or someone else. Estimate the cost in terms of packs of cigarettes and put the money aside to buy these presents.

• Keep very busy on the big day. Go to the movies, exercise, take long walks, go bike riding.

• Remind your family and friends that this is your quit date and ask them to help you over the rough spots of the first couple of days and weeks.

• Buy yourself a treat or do something special to celebrate.

After Quitting

• Develop a clean, fresh, nonsmoking environment around yourself, at work and at home. Buy yourself flowers. You may be surprised how much you can enjoy their scent now.

• The first few days after you quit, spend as much free time as possible in places where smoking isn't allowed, such as libraries, museums, theaters, department stores, and churches.

• Drink large quantities of water and fruit juice (but avoid sodas that contain caffeine.)

• Try to avoid alcohol, coffee, and other beverages that you associate with cigarette smoking.

• Strike up conversation instead of a match for a cigarette.

• If you miss the sensation of having a cigarette in your hand, play with something else, such as a pencil, a paper clip, a marble.

• If you miss having something in your mouth, try toothpicks or a fake cigarette.

Avoid Temptation

• Instead of smoking after meals, get up from the table and brush your teeth or go for a walk.

> Never allow yourself to think that "one won't hurt"— it will.

• If you always smoke while driving, listen to a particularly interesting radio program or your favorite music, or take public transportation for a while, if you can.

• For the first 1–3 weeks, avoid situations you strongly associate with the pleasurable aspects of smoking, such as watching your favorite TV program, sitting in your favorite chair, or having a cocktail before dinner.

• Until you are confident of your ability to stay off cigarettes, limit your socializing to healthful, outdoor activities or situations where smoking is not allowed.

• If you must be in a situation where you'll be tempted to smoke, such as a cocktail or dinner party, try to associate with the nonsmokers there.

• Try to analyze cigarette ads to understand how they attempt to "sell" you on individual brands.

Coping Without Cigarettes

• Keep oral substitutes handy. Try carrots, pickles, sunflower seeds, apples, celery, raisins, or sugarless gum instead of a cigarette.

• Take 10 deep breaths and hold the last one while lighting a match. Exhale slowly and blow out the match. Pretend it's a cigarette and crush it out in an ashtray.

• Take a shower or bath if possible.

• Learn to relax quickly and deeply. Make yourself limp, visualize a soothing, pleasing situation and get away from it all for a moment. Concentrate on that peaceful image and nothing else.

• Light incense or a candle instead of a cigarette.

• Never allow yourself to think that "one won't hurt"—it will.

Teens' Views on Government Anti-Tobacco Efforts

Susan Page and Wendy Koch

Federal lawmakers have proposed numerous policies to help reduce the incidence of teen smoking, including raising the price of a pack of cigarettes or requiring purchasers to show proof of age. However, many teenagers believe that they are the best judges as to which responses to teen smoking will be most effective. Susan Page and Wendy Koch, reporters for *USA Today*, present the views of several teenagers on a Senate bill that would target teen smoking.

Fawn Hast doesn't usually pay for her pack-a-day habit, bumming cigarettes from her mother and older sister. But she admits smoking has cost her a lot, from her spot on the girls' track team to her relationship with her father, "the biggest anti-smoker in the world."

She's addicted, Fawn says, and she'd like to quit. But she and many of her sophomore classmates at Fort Hill High School [in Cumberland, Maryland] doubt that the remedies being prescribed in Washington will stop most teens from smoking.

"There's no way you can really stop anyone," says Fawn, an outspoken 15-year-old who is active in the school's Sierra Club.

Adds Nick Beach, 15, a non-smoker: "If you tell kids not to do something, they'll do it more."

Government Efforts

How to prevent teen-agers from starting a lifelong tobacco habit is now the subject of fierce debate and political jockeying. Despite dire warnings from many parents and public health officials, youth smoking rates have risen nearly a third [since 1992].

[In May 1998,] the Senate [considered] a sweeping bill that would levy penalties of $516 billion on the tobacco industry over 25 years, increase the price of a cigarette pack by $1.10 and impose tough restrictions on advertising and sales. House Republican leaders are suggesting a narrower bill with fewer fines. [The measurement failed in June 1998.]

> Banning vending machines and cracking down on sales is seen as little more than an inconvenience.

Whatever their approach, members of Congress and President Clinton say their primary goal is to reduce underage smoking. The Senate bill sets a goal of reducing teen smoking by 60% over 10 years.

But drive 135 miles northwest of the capital to this bucolic, blue-collar city of 23,700 and the teen-agers make it clear how difficult this task will be—and how disconnected the Washington debate seems to be from their lives.

Teen-Agers Offer Their Views

As a reality check on what may well be the highest-profile domestic issue of the year, *USA Today* polled the sophomore class at Fort Hill High School, listened to group discussions about smoking and talked with students clustered in "smokers' alley," a patch of land across the street and off school property where a few dozen teens puff on cigarettes before and after school. A handful also use snuff.

The survey found that about one-fourth of the sophomore class smokes, with girls almost three times more likely to smoke than boys.

Nearly one-third of the smokers say they started before they were teen-agers, at age 12 or younger.

Their chief reaction to Washington's remedies, at least considered individually, was skepticism. Raising the price of cigarettes by $1.10 a pack won't deter many, though a price increase that gets a pack over $5 might. (A pack now costs about $2.) Banning vending machines and cracking down on sales is seen as little more than an inconvenience.

> Smoking clearly has become an entrenched part of teen-age culture, with an estimated 3,000 teens taking up the habit every day.

At 15 and 16, they say their smoking habits already are so entrenched that policymakers would do better to focus on their elementary-school siblings.

"They should start early," says Jamie Deans, 16, a member of the track team who says she smokes a few Marlboro Reds a day. "In preschool," adds Nicole Shaidt, 15, a pack-a-day smoker who says she started at 9 or 10.

Government Officials Respond

Senator John McCain [a Republican from Arizona], who crafted the Senate bill and is leading the effort to pass it, seems neither surprised nor deterred by the teen-agers' responses. "When we're young we think we're going to live forever," he says. "Our job is to point out to them the consequences of smoking." He notes the government has succeeded on other public health fronts with teens, increasing seat belt use and reducing drunken driving.

Health and Human Services Secretary Donna Shalala says the job won't be easy or inexpensive and may involve some trial-

and-error in policy. "The reason we're saying we need a comprehensive bill is because we don't believe that there is a silver bullet," she says.

Both speak from personal experience. Shalala started smoking at 18 and a decade later found quitting "the most difficult thing I've ever had to do in my whole life." McCain, a POW during the Vietnam War, calls kicking his two-pack-a-day, 20-year habit one of the toughest things he's ever done.

Reprinted with permission from Don Meredith.

"We don't know exactly what it is that stops kids from smoking," McCain acknowledges, noting that his bill would fund more research into the question.

Advertising and Price Increases

The research done already suggests that cigarette advertising is a powerful influence on teens. A 1994 study by the Centers for Disease Control found that the three brands young smokers buy most—Marlboro, Camel and Newport—were the three most heavily advertised.

Price also can have an impact, especially on younger teens.

The Treasury Department projects that the McCain bill's price increase would cut teen smoking by 29%, and its restrictions on access would reduce it by another 11%. Some communities report success through strict enforcement of laws barring cigarette sales to minors.

But smoking clearly has become an entrenched part of teen-age culture, with an estimated 3,000 teens taking up the habit every day. The *USA Today* poll of 202 Fort Hill sophomores, designed to be a sampling of views rather than a scientific survey, found:

> Nine out of 10 non-smokers say concern about their health is a factor in their decision to avoid the habit.

• Nearly all the smokers say they do it because it relaxes them, and more than half say they like the taste. Four in 10 say they smoke to enhance marijuana's effect. And, in a reaction that will be no surprise to many parents of teen-agers, nearly 40% say they smoke because adults tell them not to.

• One-third say free stop-smoking programs would help them quit. Parents also could help: about one in three of the student smokers say they'd stop if their parents insisted. The proposed $1.10 per pack price increase would prompt 14% to stop; a price hike of $1.50 would deter 23%.

Ineffective Approaches

But other measures in the McCain bill were dismissed as irrelevant by most of the student smokers. Almost all of them say banning vending machines and requiring proof of age to buy cigarettes wouldn't matter; they say they get cigarettes from parents or older friends. They generally dismiss the idea that a celebrity advertising campaign against smoking would have much effect.

And a bigger warning label?

Fawn Hast laughs at the idea. "Sometimes I stare at the warning label while I'm smoking," she says, demonstrating a languid smoker's pose. The health consequences of smoking already have gotten through: 100% of those surveyed say they believe smoking will hurt their health.

Health Concerns

That has helped persuade many students not to smoke. Nine out of 10 non-smokers say concern about their health is a factor in their decision to avoid the habit. About six in 10 of the non-smokers report having a close relative or friend who suffers from a smoking-related disease.

Nathan Curry, 15, says his grandfather smoked most of his life. "Now he can't walk a few steps without wheezing," he says, shaking his head. Trapper Duckworth, 15, says his uncle "will come up 20 feet to my house and he'll be all out of breath, saying, 'Can I have a cigarette?'" Both teens are non-smokers.

Among non-smokers, strong majorities say they don't like the smell or the taste of cigarettes. A majority mention parental opposition as a factor. And about 70% of boys worry it would hurt them in sports.

The school has a strict no-smoking policy, and Cumberland police officers sometimes hand out $25 citations to underage smokers. A student found in possession of cigarettes gets an automatic three-day in-school suspension. A five-time offender is likely to be removed from the school.

The Influence of Friends and Family

Many of the smokers say they started because their friends did. "To fit in with the crowd," recalls Heather Wilt, 15, who started smoking Newports three years ago. Most of the smokers say they have a parent who smokes, although so do some of the non-smokers.

Once they started, the teen-agers say, it's hard to stop. About half the smokers say they want to quit, including almost three-fourths of the boys. Two-thirds of the teen smokers predict they will quit some day.

Fawn has tried to quit smoking several times since starting at 12 or 13, only to relapse when she feels stressed and shaky. "I become very mean" when not smoking, she says ruefully. "I'm just not a nice person to be around."

She scolds her 13-year-old sister, Casey, for occasionally snitching a cigarette from their mother. "I tell her all the time I wish I never did it," she says. At the moment, their 11-year-old twin sisters, Mandy and Mindy, are smoke-free.

But some of the twins' friends have already started to smoke.

Teens Can Take Action

Patricia Sosa

Peer influence is a major factor in teenagers' lives. This influence can be negative, as when friends encourage one another to smoke. However, teens can also play an important role in ending the problem of teen smoking. They can advocate restrictions on tobacco sales, teach fellow teens about the health risks of smoking, or lobby Congress for tougher laws. Patricia Sosa, director of constituency relations for the Campaign for Tobacco-Free Kids, notes some of the efforts made by teenagers throughout the United States.

K ids are Big Tobacco's number one target—and they are quickly becoming its number one enemy.

The past few years have seen a dramatic surge in youth advocacy, as kids all over America have come to realize that they are not merely victims and not merely part of the problem. They can also be a powerful part of the solution, and many of them are.

Increased Activism

Consider, for example, the tremendous rise in participation in Kick Butts Day, the annual opportunity for US kids to engage in activities that put the tobacco companies on notice that they will no longer tolerate being lured into smoking through slick adver-

Excerpted from Patricia Sosa, "Kids Kicking Butts," *Christian Social Action*, June 1998. Reprinted with permission from *Christian Social Action* magazine.

tising campaigns and giveaways. Sponsored jointly by the Campaign for Tobacco-free Kids and New York City Public Advocate Mark Green, this once-yearly national youth activists' day spiked to a record 400-plus events in April [1998], up from 82 events in 1997.

All over America, young people organized rallies on their state capitol steps, lobbied for increases in tobacco excise taxes, pushed for local ordinances to ban cigarette vending machines, applied pressure to restaurants to prohibit smoking for diners, and conducted mock funerals and trials for Mr. Butts in a show of protest for the way the tobacco industry has profited at the expense of their health.

> Kids . . . are quickly becoming [Big Tobacco's] number one enemy.

"In 1997, America's kids showed they have a powerful voice in the fight against tobacco," said campaign President Bill Novelli. "This year, that voice has grown even louder."

These young people were not alone. While they took the initiative, planned the events and came up with creative new ways to strike back against the industry, they were joined in cities and towns across the country by adult community activists, local elected officials, state attorneys general, congressmen and senators, and representatives from 17 federal agencies. No less than six Cabinet members and Vice President Al Gore all took part in Kick Butts Day activities around the nation to let US children know that the country's adults were standing behind them.

This is just one way that this country's young people are joining the front lines of this crucial public health battle.

Teens Who Made a Difference

Numerous teens spend their free time year-round devising new ways to counter the tobacco industry's powerful influence on their peers. Every year, the campaign recognizes the country's top young tobacco control activists with the Youth Advocates of

the Year Awards, a national honor bestowed during a gala cele-
bration in Washington, D.C., and attended by the movers and
shakers of the tobacco control movement.

Anna Markee, the campaign's 1997 National Youth Advocate
of the Year, explained what motivates her and other young
people to commit to this cause. "For decades, the tobacco industry has been profiting at our expense," she said. "But now we
are fighting back. Eventually, they'll learn that our lungs are not
for sale."

On April 30, 1998, the campaign recognized five regional
Youth Advocates, a national winner and the first-ever group
winner as 1998 Youth Advocates of the Year. These young activists will continue to work with the campaign throughout the
coming year to push for comprehensive national tobacco control
legislation and other policy changes that can save kids' lives.

Examples of Activism

Here are just a few of the achievements cited by the campaign
when recognizing this year's winners:

• Emily Broxterman, 16, of Overland Park, Kansas, each year
helps to organize an annual march and rally at her state capitol
to mobilize young people from all across Kansas to push for
tougher tobacco control laws. She works
with local merchants to encourage them
to make it tougher for minors to purchase tobacco products, testifies before
the state legislature and travels to local
schools speaking to younger students
about the harmful effects of tobacco use.
Emily is the campaign's 1998 National
Youth Advocate of the Year.

> Numerous teens
> spend their free time
> year-round devising
> new ways to counter
> the tobacco indus-
> try's powerful influ-
> ence on their peers.

• Michael Higgins, 13, of Monroeville, New Jersey, helped to
draft and push through a local ordinance banning vending machines in his home township. The ordinance was then used as a

model by other towns in his county. His current goal is to pass a county-wide ban. Michael is the campaign's 1998 East Regional Youth Advocate of the Year.

• Deanna Durrett, 16, of Louisville, Kentucky, testified before the Kentucky House of Representatives, urging its members to adopt tougher tobacco control policies statewide. To help her peers learn how to contact their legislators and how to lobby for tougher laws to reduce teen smoking, she organized a rally on her state capitol steps. Two hundred of her fellow teens showed

> Children are taking their first tentative puffs on a cigarette before they graduate from elementary school.

up. Deanna is the campaign's 1998 South Regional Youth Advocate of the Year.

• Gretchen Sneegas, 11, of Indianapolis, Indiana, organized a protest outside her state capitol building after the state legislature overrode former Governor Evan Bayh's veto of legislation that took away the right of local governments to restrict the sale of tobacco products to minors. Later, she took up the charge for a statewide ban on cigarette vending machines. Gretchen is the campaign's 1998 Midwest Region Youth Advocate of the Year.

• Amanda Tunnell, 16, of Oklahoma City, Oklahoma, testified in support of a bill that allows Oklahoma cities to license tobacco retailers and fine those caught selling tobacco products to minors. Her concern about secondhand smoke and how it affects people like her mother, who has asthma, inspired her to survey local restaurants and encourage more of them to provide a smoke-free environment for customers. Amanda is the campaign's 1998 Central Region Youth Advocate of the Year.

• Annie Aguilar, 17, of Alhambra, California, spoke before Members of Congress about the prevalence of tobacco ads to which kids are subjected on a daily basis and created a guidebook and video to teach other kids how to become tobacco control advocates. Annie is the campaign's 1998 West Regional

Youth Advocate of the Year.

• The S.H.O.C.K. Coalition (Saving the Health of Our Communities and Kids), a group of close to 40 teens from Brooklyn, New York, collected 4,200 signatures and 3,000 letters in support of the Youth Protection Against Tobacco Advertising and Promotion Act, which made it illegal to place tobacco advertising within 1,000 feet of any school, playground or child care facility in the five boroughs of New York City. The S.H.O.C.K. Coalition is the campaign's first-ever winner of the Group Youth Advocates of the Year Award.

"These young people have accomplished a great deal," Novelli said. "Their outstanding efforts to motivate their peers, mobilize legislators and prevent new generations from tobacco addiction are truly remarkable."

Additional Efforts

In addition to the Youth Advocates of the Year Awards, the campaign has begun several other initiatives to encourage involvement from kids and communities in the fight for a smoke-free environment for children. This year, the campaign is expanding its youth advocacy outreach by working in partnership with the Public Relations Society of America (PRSA) in 12 pilot projects across the country. PRSA members are paired with young people anxious to learn the tools of advocacy and public relations, and these highly motivated professionals are working with them to teach them those tools.

The campaign also offers opportunities to adults who want to join the "tobacco wars." It recently created a National Action Network of 12,000 activists from across the country. These crucial "field workers" are called upon to write letters to their congressmen and senators supporting critical legislation and to take an active role in pushing for initiatives that will help reduce teen smoking.

At any given time, there are countless other tobacco control efforts taking place all across the nation, sponsored by campaign partners, such as the American Heart Association, American Cancer Society and others. Still, much remains to be done.

Never before has the need for involvement been so great. Despite all of these efforts, by thousands of committed activists, smoking among high school seniors today has reached a 19-year high, more than one in three seniors smokes. Every day, 6,000 teenagers pick up a cigarette for the first time, and 3,000 of them become regular, daily smokers. A third of those new smokers will die prematurely from tobacco-related disease.

Sadly, the average kid begins smoking at age 13, meaning many start much earlier. Children are taking their first tentative puffs on a cigarette before they graduate from elementary school.

These figures may seem daunting, but [1998] holds the best opportunity yet to reduce substantially teen smoking and start driving those numbers down.

Bibliography

Books

William Everett Bailey — *The Invisible Drug*. Cincinnati, OH: Mosaic, 1996.

Janet Brigham — *Dying to Quit: Why We Smoke and How We Stop*. Washington, DC: Joseph Henry Press, 1998.

John Fahs — *Cigarette Confidential: The Unfiltered Truth About the Ultimate American Addiction*. New York: Berkeley, 1996.

Philip J. Hilts — *Smoke Screen: The Truth Behind the Tobacco Industry Cover-Up*. Reading, MA: Addison Wesley, 1996.

Peter D. Jacobson — *Tobacco Control Laws: Implementation and Enforcement*. Santa Monica, CA: RAND, 1997.

Elizabeth Keyishian — *Everything You Need to Know About Smoking*. New York: Rosen, 1997.

Edward L. Koven — *Smoking: The Story Behind the Haze*. Commack, NY: Kroshka Books, 1998.

Rachel Kranz — *Straight Talk About Smoking*. New York: FactsOnFile, 1999.

Susan S. Lang and Beth H. Marks	*Teens and Tobacco: A Fatal Attraction.* New York: Twenty-First Century Books, 1996.
Daniel McMillan	*Teen Smoking: Understanding the Risk.* Springfield, NJ: Enslow, 1997.
Laurence Pringle	*Smoking: A Risky Business.* New York: Morrow Junior Books, 1996.
Jacob Sullum	*For Your Own Good: The Anti-Smoking Crusade and the Tyranny of Public Health.* New York: Free Press, 1998.

Periodicals

Jonathan Alter	"Smoking Out What's Cool," *Newsweek,* June 30, 1997.
Consumer Reports	"Hooked on Tobacco: The Teen Epidemic," March 1995.
Fabiola Duvalsaint	"Why We Smoke: Quitting Is a Drag," *New Youth Connections,* September/October 1997. Available from 144 West 26th St., 8th Floor, New York, NY 10001.
FDA Consumer Magazine	"Young People Talk with FDA Commissioner About Smoking," January/February 1996.
Ginny Graves	"Teen Smoking: Helping Kids Quit," *American Health for Women,* January/February 1997.

Jane Gross — "Young Blacks Link Tobacco Use to Marijuana," *New York Times*, April 22, 1998.

Issues and Controversies On File — "Tobacco Settlement," November 20, 1998. Available from FactsOnFile News Services, 11 Penn Plaza, New York, NY 10001-2006.

Kathiann Kowalski — "Tobacco's Toll on Teens," *Current Health*, February 1997.

Robert A. Levy and Rosalind B. Marimont — "Lies, Damned Lies, and 400,000 Smoking-Related Deaths," *Regulation*, vol. 21, no. 4, 1998. Available from 1000 Massachusetts Ave. NW, Washington, DC 10002.

John J. Lynch and Thomas Humber — "Do We Need a Tobacco Bill?" *World & I*, July 1998. Available from 3600 New York Ave. NE, Washington, DC 20002.

Laura Mansnerus — "Don't Smoke. Please. Pretty Please." *New York Times*, September 15, 1996.

Debbie Martin-Morris — "Why Smoking's a Real Drag!" *'Teen*, January 1998.

John McCain — "A Defeat for the Nation's Children," *America*, August 15–22, 1998.

Barry Meier — "Politics of Youth Smoking Fueled by Unproven Data," *New York Times*, May 20, 1998.

Mark Naymik — "After Joe Camel," *Washington Post National Weekly Edition*, September 22, 1997.

Yumiko Ono	"Teenagers Tell Which Antismoking Ads Work," *Wall Street Journal*, August 30, 1995.
Mark Peyser	"Cool Fools," *Newsweek*, July 21, 1997.
John P. Pierce et al.	"Tobacco Industry Promotion of Cigarettes and Adolescent Smoking," *Journal of the American Medical Association*, February 18, 1998. Available from 515 North State St., Chicago, IL 60610.
Dennis Prager	"The Soul-Corrupting Anti-Tobacco Crusade," *Weekly Standard*, July 20, 1998. Available from PO Box 96153, Washington, DC 20090-6153.
John Schwartz	"Stop Smoking? Like Yeah. Right. Whatever." *Washington Post National Weekly Edition*, November 10, 1997.
Geoffrey Stevens	"Stopping Kids from Smoking," *Maclean's*, August 24, 1998.
Jacob Sullum	"Cowboys, Camels, and Kids: Does Advertising Turn People into Smokers?" *Reason*, April 1998.
Mike Thomas	"Just Trying to Be Cool," *Reader's Digest*, March 1997.
Richard L. Worsnop	"Teens and Tobacco," *CQ Researcher*, December 1, 1995. Available from 1414 22nd St. NW, Washington, DC 20037.

Organizations and Websites

The editors have compiled the following list of organizations concerned with the issues debated in this book. The descriptions are derived from matcrials provided by the organizations. All have publications or information available for interested readers. The list was compiled on the date of publication of the present volume; the information provided here may change. Be aware that many organizations take several weeks or longer to respond to inquiries, so allow as much time as possible.

Action on Smoking and Health (ASH)

2013 H St. NW, Washington, DC 20006
(202) 659-4310
website: www.ash.org

Action on Smoking and Health promotes the rights of non-smokers and works to protect thcm from the harms of smoking. ASH worked to eliminate tobacco ads from radio and television. The organization publishes thc bimonthly newsletter *ASH Smoking and Health Review* and fact sheets on a variety of topics, including tccn smoking.

American Cancer Society

1599 Clifton Road NE, Atlanta, GA 30329
(800) ACS-2345 (227-2345)
website: www.cancer.org

The American Cancer Society is devoted to educating the public about cancer and to funding cancer research. The society educates the public about the dangers of smoking and on lobbying for antismoking legislation. The American Cancer Society makes available hundreds of publications.

American Council on Science and Health (ACSH)
1995 Broadway, 2nd Floor, New York, NY 10023-5860
(212) 362-7044 • fax: (212) 362-4919
e-mail: acsh@acsh.org • website: www.acsh.org

ACSH is a consumer education group concerned with issues related to food, nutrition, chemicals, pharmaceuticals, lifestyle, the environment, and health. It publishes the quarterly newsletter *Priorities* as well as the booklets *The Tobacco Industry's Use of Nicotine as a Drug* and *Marketing Cigarettes to Kids*.

Americans for Nonsmokers' Rights
2530 San Pablo Ave., Suite J, Berkeley, CA 94702
(510) 841-3032 • fax: (510) 841-3071
e-mail: anr@no-smoke.org • website: www.no-smoke.org

Americans for Nonsmokers' Rights seeks to protect the rights of nonsmokers in public settings. It works with the American Nonsmokers' Rights Foundation, which promotes nonsmokers' rights, and public education about involuntary smoking. The organization publishes the quarterly newsletter *ANR Update* and the guidebook *How to Butt In: Teens Take Action*.

American Smokers Alliance (ASA)
PO Box 189, Bellvue, CO 80512
fax: (970) 493-4253
e-mail: derf@smokers.org • website: www.smokers.org

The American Smokers Alliance is a nonprofit organization of volunteers who believe that nonsmokers and smokers have equal rights. ASA strives to fight discrimination against smokers in the workplace, and it publishes articles and news bulletins, including *Smokers Have Reduced Risks of Alzheimer's and Parkinson's Disease.*

Canadian Council for Tobacco Control (CCTC)

170 Laurier Ave. W, Suite 1000, Ottawa, ON K1P 5V5 CANADA
(800) 267-5234 • (613) 567-3050 • fax: (613) 567-5695
e-mail: info-services@cctc.ca • website: www.cctc.ca/ncth

The CCTC works to ensure a healthier society, free from addiction and involuntary exposure to tobacco products. It promotes a comprehensive tobacco control program involving educational, social, fiscal, and legislative interventions. It publishes several fact sheets, including *Promoting a Lethal Product.*

Fight Ordinances & Restrictions to Control & Eliminate Smoking (FORCES)

PO Box 591257, San Francisco, CA 94159
(415) 824-4716
e-mail: info@forces.org • website: www.forces.org

FORCES fights against smoking ordinances and restrictions designed to eventually eliminate smoking, and it works to increase public awareness of smoking-related legislation. Although FORCES does not advocate smoking, it asserts that an individual has the right to choose to smoke. FORCES publishes *Tobacco Weekly* as well as many articles.

KidsHealth.org

The Nemours Foundation Center for Children's Health Media
1600 Rockland Rd., Wilmington, DE 19803
(302) 651-4046 • fax: (302) 651-4077
e-mail: info@KidsHealth.org • website: www.KidsHealth.org

The mission of KidsHealth.org is to help families make informed decisions about children's health by creating the highest quality health media. Its teen section covers a wide variety of issues, including teen smoking. *How to Raise Non-Smoking Kids* and *Smoking: Cutting Through the Hype* are two of its numerous publications.

National Center for Tobacco-Free Kids/Campaign for Tobacco-Free Kids

1707 L St. NW, Suite 800, Washington, DC 20036
(800) 284-KIDS (284-5437)
e-mail: info@tobaccofreekids.org
website: www.tobaccofreekids.org

The National Center for Tobacco-Free Kids/Campaign for Tobacco-Free Kids is the largest private initiative ever launched to protect children from tobacco addiction. The Center works in partnership with the American Cancer Society, American Medical Association, and over one hundred other health, civic, corporate, youth, and religous organizations. Among the center's publications are fact sheets, including *Tobacco Use Among Youth* and *Tobacco Marketing to Kids.*

Stop Teenage Addiction to Tobacco (STAT)

Northeastern University
360 Huntington Ave., 241 Cushing Hall, Boston, MA 02115
(617) 373-7828 • fax: (617) 369-0130
e-mail: info@stat.org • website: www.stat.org

STAT is a national organization whose mission is to end children and teenage addiction to tobacco. Its tobacco awareness and prevention programs rely heavily on youth participation. STAT publishes a variety of fact sheets as well as educational and training material.

Tobacco-Related Disease Research Program (TRDRP)
Office of Health Affairs
University of California, Office of the President
300 Lakeside Dr., 6th Floor, Oakland, CA 94612-3550
(510) 987-9870 • fax: (510) 835-4740
e-mail: TRDRP@ucop.edu.
website: www.ucop.cdu/srphome/trdrp/welcome.html

The TRDRP is an organization that funds and encourages research that focuses on the causes, prevention, and treatment of tobacco-related diseases and on how to reduce the costs of tobacco use in California. It publishes annual reports and a quarterly newsletter.

U.S. Food and Drug Administration (FDA)
Rockville, MD 20857
(800) 532-4440 • (301) 443-1130 • fax: (301) 443-9767
e-mail: execsec@oc.fda.gov • website: www.fda.gov

As the agency of the U.S. government charged with protecting the health of the public against impure and unsafe foods, drugs, cosmetics, and other potential hazards, the FDA has sought the regulation of nicotine as a drug and has investigated manipulation of nicotine levels in cigarettes by the tobacco industry. It provides copies of congressional testimony given in the debate over the regulation of nicotine.

Websites

CyberIsle
www.cyberisle.org
This site features information and advice on teen smoking.

Teen Advice Center
www.geocities.com/SouthBeach/Boardwalk/6384/
This site provides advice on issues that affects teens, such as school, sexuality, drugs, and smoking.

Index

Aaron, Hank, 95–96
Action on Smoking and Health, 102,
103–105
Addiction (M.A. Jarvis), 105
adult smokers, 9, 15, 19, 99–100,
123
advertising, cigarette
bans on, 12, 14, 44–46, 108, 129
on billboards, 14, 33–34, 47
claimed smoking was healthy, 10
does not cause teen smoking, 16,
47–50, 59, 76
featured celebrities, 10
government regulation of, 15–16
in magazines, 13–14, 33, 76, 94
money spent on, 17
success of, 11, 13, 14, 45, 121
targets
African Americans, 39
teenagers, 12–14, 20–21, 34,
43–47, 125
women, 10–11, 14, 98
teen activists against, 125–30
African American smokers, 21, 56,
101
decrease in by teenagers, 41
increase in, 37–41
lung cancer deaths of, 38
marijuana use of, 39–40
targeted by tobacco industry, 39
Aguilar, Annie, 128–29
alcohol addiction, 103–106
America (magazine), 43
American Cancer Society, 62, 65, 96
American Council on Science and
Health, 83, 91
American Lung Association, 88

American Tobacco Company, 11
Amosa, Amanda, 10–11
antismoking activists, 125–30
apomorphine, 103–104
aveena sativa, 103

Battle, Brandi, 51–53, 58, 59
Baxter, Susan, 30
Bayh, Evan, 128
Beach, Nick, 119
Bearman, Mary, 75
billboards, 14, 33–34, 47
black teens. *See* African American
smokers
Bloch, Michele, 31
blood circulation, 89
Boodman, Sandra G., 98
Botvin, Gilbert, 21
Bradley, Nickita, 51, 52, 54–55, 59
Brain, Marshall, 24
brain functions, 62
Brigham, Janet, 19
Brodish, Paul H., 83
bronchitis, chronic, 11
Broughton, Trenée Bryant, 77–81
Brown and Williamson tobacco
company, 13, 39
Broxterman, Emily, 127

California, 20
Camel cigarettes, 9, 10, 12–14, 21,
39, 121
see also Joe Camel
Campaign for Tobacco-Free Kids,
12, 126–30
cancer, 11, 96, 97
and smokeless tobacco, 94, 95

see also lung cancer
candy cigarettes, 68
carbon monoxide, 54, 65, 90
Centers for Disease Control and
  Prevention, 9, 56, 84, 85
  on African American smokers, 37,
    40–41
  on cigarette advertising, 121
  on smokeless tobacco, 95
Chatelaine (magazine), 34
chewing tobacco. *See* smokeless
  tobacco
chronic obstructive pulmonary
  disease (COPD), 86–87
cigarettes. *See* smoking
*Cigarettes: What the Warning Label
  Doesn't Tell You* (ACSH), 91
cigarette vending machines, 120,
  127–28
cigars, 41
Clinton, Bill, 15, 44, 119
Cloninger, Robert, 23
cocaine, 32, 40, 62, 102, 105
contraceptives, 88
Coronary Artery Risk Development
  in Young Adults (CARDIA),
  100–101
Cox, William J., 46
Curry, Nathan, 123

Deans, Jamie, 120
DiMaggio, Joe, 10
DNA, 88
Doll, Richard, 107
drug use, 32, 39–41, 62, 102–103,
  105
Duckworth, Trapper, 123
Durrett, Deanna, 128

Eastridge, Eileen, 74
Eastridge, Jeff, 72–76
eating disorders, 31–32
Eisner, J.R., 23
emphysema, 64, 86
Environmental Protection Agency,
79
Eysenck, Hans, 108–109

Federal Cigarette Labeling and
  Advertising Act, 11–12
Federal Drug Administration, 15
female smokers, 30–36, 87, 88, 120
  and pregnancy, 54–55, 67, 88, 90
  want to
    appear grown-up, 30–33
    control weight, 10–11, 14, 30,
      98–101
French, Simone A., 100
Frist, Bill, 51–52, 57–60
Frost, Mimi, 30

Garagiola, Joe, 95–96
Gardiner, Phillip, 37
Gilligan, Carol, 32
Gore, Al, 126
Greaves, Lorraine, 32, 35–36
Green, Mark, 126

Hachey, Dawn, 30–31
Haglund, Margaretha, 10–11
Hamilton, Wanda, 16
Hast, Fawn, 118–19, 122, 124
Hatton, Judith, 102, 105
Health Canada, 30–31, 35, 36
heart disease, 64, 88–89
heroin, 62, 102, 103, 105
Higgins, Michael, 127–28
Hispanic smokers, 21, 38, 40–41, 56

*International Journal of Eating
  Disorders*, 32
Izenberg, Neil, 96, 97

Jackson, Christine, 22
Jarvis, M.A., 105
Jensen, Phyllis, 32
Joe Camel, 13–15, 33, 45–46, 47
Jolly, Kellie, 51, 52, 53–54, 59–60
Josh, 51, 52, 55–57
Journal of the American Medical

Association, 10, 12, 43, 45, 48

Kick Butts Day, 125–26
KidsHealth.org, 93
Klesges, Robert C., 98–99
Koch, Wendy, 118
Kool cigarettes, 39
Koop, C. Everett, 102

Lucky Strike cigarettes, 11
lung cancer, 11, 64, 65, 87–88
  in African American men, 38
  from secondhand smoke, 79
lung functioning, 86–87, 90

Macara, Sandy, 106
magazine ads, 13–14, 33, 76, 94
marijuana, 32, 39–41, 62
Markee, Anna, 127
Marlboro cigarettes, 11, 12, 21, 33,
  39, 76, 121
Mâsse, Louise, 23
McCain, John, 15–16, 120–22
Mermelstein, Robin, 39
Minna, John, 65
mouth cancer, 96, 97
Murphy, Patricia J., 61

National Cancer Institute, 111
National Spit Tobacco Education
  Program (NSTEP), 95–96
Native American smokers, 9, 38
nervous system, 62, 104–105
Newport cigarettes, 12, 39, 121
nicotine, 39, 40, 54
  addictive effects of, 62–63, 85, 95,
    102–105
  compared to heroin, 62, 102, 103
  as a drug, 45
  is not a drug, 105–109
  in smokeless tobacco, 94, 96
nicotine patches, 35
Non-Smokers' Rights Association,
  35
Novak, Amanda, 16

Novelli, Bill, 126, 129
Novello, Antonia C., 66

Page, Susan, 118
Pellizzer, Sandy, 34–35
Philip Morris, 11, 14, 46
Pierce, John P., 20, 48–50
Pollay, Richard, 32–33
Pray, Dale, 67–71
pregnancy, 54–55, 67, 88, 90
prescription drugs, 105–106
Public Relations Society of America
  (PRSA), 129

Reagan, Ronald, 10
Reason (magazine), 16, 43
respiratory illnesses, 11, 86
R.J. Reynolds Tobacco Company, 9,
  12, 14, 15, 39, 45
Rohde, Paul, 22
Rowley, Christine H., 14–15

Salem cigarettes, 39
San Diego Union-Tribune
  (newspaper), 48
Schilling, Curt, 96
Scholastic Update (magazine), 16
secondhand smoke, 68, 78–81
Selin, Heather, 35
Shaidt, Nicole, 120
Shalala, Donna, 120–21
S.H.O.C.K. (Saving the Health of
  Our Communities and Kids), 129
Simpson, Kevin, 72
skin wrinkles, 90
Skoal, 12–13
smokeless tobacco, 12–13, 20,
  93–97
  damage caused by, 95–97
  ingredients in, 94
  quitting, 96–97
Smokeless Tobacco Council, 94
*Smoke Screen: Women's Smoking
  and Social Control* (Greaves), 35
smoking

adult, 9, 15, 19, 99–100, 123
bans on, 44, 80, 119, 123
beginning age for, 25, 31, 44, 71,
    75, 85, 120, 130
cutting down, 64–66, 76, 113–15
deaths from, 61, 71, 79, 85
deciding against
    due to pregnancy, 54–55
    for health reasons, 52, 53, 64, 123
    for religious reasons, 19–20, 53
    too expensive, 64
    want to be good athlete, 53–54,
        60, 123
    would be criticized, 77, 123
enhances marijuana use, 39, 122
government deterrents to, 119–20,
    122
health effects from, 11, 28, 46–47,
    61–62, 64, 83–92
increase in, 38, 84, 119, 122, 130
is not drug dependency, 105–109
laws regarding, 11, 35, 122
linked to promotional merchandise,
    13–14, 20, 45, 49, 58
in movies, 14–15, 33, 108
parental disapproval of, 56–57, 74
prevalence of, 9, 16, 19, 61, 130
quitting, 28, 54, 57, 66, 71, 122
    cessation programs, 63, 64, 75,
        105
    difficulty of, 73, 75–76, 85,
        112–13, 123–24
    does not eliminate health risks,
        84, 87–88, 91
    health benefits from, 65, 85–87
    preparing for, 111–15
    success rate, 84, 85, 92, 104, 107
    tips for, 113–17
    uncertainty about, 72–75
    weight gain from, 99, 101
reasons for, 109
    to appear grown-up, 24, 25, 30,
        31, 32, 33
    to control weight, 10–11, 14, 30,
        98–101

due to
    depression, 22, 31
    feelings of incompetency, 22
    immaturity, 26, 27, 29
    parental behaviors, 22
    personality styles, 23
easy to obtain, 56, 69
enhances effects of marijuana, 39,
    122
enjoyable, 23, 30, 56, 122
following parents' example, 34,
    53, 60, 68, 69
need to rebel, 10, 24–25, 64, 122
peer pressure, 21–23, 53–56, 58,
    70, 73–74
relaxing, 23, 62, 64, 79, 105, 122
wanting to fit in, 24, 31, 62,
    69–71, 73, 123
reversing damage from, 84
teenage, 44
will not control weight, 98–101
see also nicotine
Smoking and Common Sense (Voss),
    106
Sneegas, Gretchen, 128
snuff, 94
SOS (Stop Our Smoking), 63, 64
Sosa, Patricia, 125
spit tobacco. See smokeless tobacco
sports idols, 10, 95–96
Sullum, Jacob, 16, 42
Supreme Court, 15
Surgeon General, 38, 94–96, 102,
    104
surgeon general warnings, 10–11
Sussman, Steve, 21
Sutton, Charyn, 39–40

teen smokers. See African American
    smokers; female smokers; Hispanic
    smokers; white smokers
Terry, Luther L., 11
tetrahydrocannabinol (THC), 40
tobacco, 9, 15, 62–63
    see also nicotine

Tobacco Control (journal), 10
tobacco industry, 9, 33, 102
  government regulation of, 35, 46,
    119, 127–29
  lawsuits against, 15, 43
  promotional merchandise of,
    13–14, 20, 48, 58
  sponsorships of, 14, 15, 34, 43
  Supreme Court rulings on, 44–45
  targets African Americans, 39
  teen critics of, 125–30
  see also advertising, cigarette
Tonkin, Roger, 31
Tremblay, Richard, 23
Tunnell, Amanda, 128
Tuttle, Bill, 95–96

USA Today (newspaper), 119, 122
United States
  Department of Health and Human
    Services, 44
  Food and Drug Administration, 44
  Senate, 11, 15–16, 51, 119
Utah, 19–20

vending machines, 44, 120, 127–28
Virginia Slims cigarettes, 11, 14
Voss, Tage, 106

Wall Street Journal (newspaper),
  12–13
Warburton, David, 23
Ward, Kenneth D., 99, 101
Washington Post (newspaper), 47
Waxman, Henry A., 45
weight control, 10–11, 14, 30
  smoking does not help, 98–101
What Doctors Don't Tell You, 106
White, Kathy, 63, 66
white smokers, 21, 38, 40, 41, 56,
  101
Wilt, Heather, 123
Women, Tobacco and the Media
  (Canadian study), 33

Youth Advocates of the Year awards,
  126–29